Breaking The Loop

Personal Growth for the Scapegoat
Beyond the Narcissistic Family System

by *Florentyna Domanski*

Copyright

Copyright © 2023 by *Florentyna Domanski*. All rights reserved. No part of this book may be reproduced, distributed, or transmitted in any form or by any means, including photocopying, recording, or other electronic or mechanical methods, without the prior written permission of the publisher. For permissions requests, please contact the publisher at artflorentyna.com.

Cover Design by *enlezLab*

Typeset and Layout by *enlezLab*

ISBN: 978-1-7776512-8-2

Disclaimer

Please be advised that this book is the product of the author's personal experience with narcissistic abuse. The author has collected information from various sources but does not claim legal ownership over any of it. This book is intended solely for the purpose of sharing the author's personal insights and is not to be used as a substitute for professional help or advice. Readers are advised to seek guidance from a qualified healthcare provider for any individualized medical advice or treatment.

The author of this book is not a licensed mental health professional and cannot provide medical advice or therapy. The information contained in this book should not be used for diagnosis or treatment of any medical condition, including Narcissistic Personality Disorder. It is highly recommended that readers seek the professional advice of qualified healthcare providers for any concerns about their individual health or mental well-being.

Readers should use their discretion when reading this book and should not rely solely on the information presented herein to make any personal decisions. The author assumes no liability for any damages, losses or claims arising from the use or interpretation of the information contained in this book.

Foreword

So, I finally did it. I walked away. I officially rejected the role of the family scapegoat - the carrier of the family's dysfunction and shame, the lowest-ranking family member, the failure, the disrupter of peace, the bad character, the ungrateful, the too sensitive, the irrational, the traitor, the problem, the burden, and the one who couldn't conform to the family's "culture". Oh, we scapegoats have been given many labels, haven't we?

I once found myself at the bottom of the 'food chain'—battling limiting beliefs about my worth, questioning my capabilities, and carrying a false sense of responsibility where the goalpost of 'peace, acceptance, respect, being heard, being seen, and being loved' continually shifted, no matter how hard I tried. When I finally made the decision to break the loop and embarked on a journey of self-discovery, introspection, and education, I realized the profound extent to which these false narratives had controlled every aspect of my life.

My journey led me to a profound realization: I wasn't the problem, and my personality didn't require perpetual fixing or changing for there to be healthy love, genuine peace, emotional safety, acceptance, and loving relationships in my life.

Instead of persisting in a cycle where I was consistently told that I needed to perpetually fix and change who I was like a broken record, I redirected my focus to listen to my needs for the first time. Creating a safe space within me, I allowed my voice to exist and be validated—by me. Choosing to prioritize my own well-being, I embarked on the ongoing restoration of my authentic self.

Breaking free from the scapegoated role is a long and difficult process, but it brings a profound sense of vindication as one reclaims autonomy and breaks free from the normalized dysfunction that rules the family system. It's empowering to reach a point of radical acceptance, take charge of one's life, pursue personal goals, find inner peace, and live a fulfilling existence beyond the pain of the past. To do so, it's essential to recognize that birth order and family ties do not define one's identity or destiny.

The purpose of this book is to help guide those who need it on their journey towards self-discovery, personal development, inner peace, and healing after leaving behind a narcissistic family system. I have provided the tools that I personally used for my own personal growth throughout the process of breaking away from my scapegoated role. The hope is that the contents of this book will empower readers to take control of their own narrative and take necessary steps to ensure that history does not repeat itself.

Ours is the tale of the scapegoat who rose from the ashes and emerged victorious. A true warrior's journey, deserving of a fairy-tale ending, where they lived happily ever after.

Florentyna Domanski

Written by a survivor for survivors, this book offers a roadmap for those who have taken the courageous step of going no contact with their narcissistic family system and embarking on the journey of recovery. The decision to sever ties with a toxic family can be painful and frightening, but it is often the only way to break the cycle of abuse and reclaim one's sense of self.

Contents

1 A Glossary about Narcissistic Family Systems — 1
Healthy Vs. Narcissistic Families 2
Recognizing a Narcissistic Personality 4
The Subtypes of Narcissism 7
Children's Family Roles 11
The Enablers 12
Narcissistic Supply 17
Gaslighting 19
Triangulation 20
Smear Campaigns 24
Emotional Incest 24
Enmeshment 25
Parentification 26
Infantilizing 27
Cognitive Dissonance 28
How To Think of Your Situation As the Family Scapegoat 29

2 Behind Closed Doors: Seeing No Evil, Hearing No Evil — 33
Deflecting Responsibility: The Martyr Syndrome 36
The Masks They Wear 37
Beneath the Mask of Worry: Covert Manipulation Tactics 39
Journal Prompts 40
The Lessons Learned 41

3 Conditional vs Unconditional Love — 45
The "Love" Experience for the Family Scapegoat 45
When Love Is a Poisoned Apple 48
Conditional Love Vs. Unconditional Love .. 48
Safe Vs Unsafe People 50
About Forgiveness 53
Journal Prompts 55
The Lessons Learned 56

4 Gaslighting — 59
When Gaslighted, You May Experience: ... 62
The Gaslighter's Toolkit 64
Techniques to "un"gaslight Yourself 65
Catching Yourself in a Loop of Repetitive Negative and Anxiety-Causing Thoughts 67
Journal Prompts 71
The Lessons Learned 71

5 Boundaries — 73
About Boundaries 78
Non-Negotiables 80
Advocating for Oneself Healthily 82
Journal Prompts 85
The Lessons Learned 86

6 The Gray Rock Method — 87
What to Expect from a Narcissist When You Lay Down Boundaries 88
How to Gray Rock 89
The Yellow Rock Method 91
Reject the Energy That You Do Not Want in Your Orbit 91
No Magic Cure to Change Narcissism 93
In the Aftermath 95
Journal Prompts 96
The Lessons Learned 97

7 The Toxic Cycles That Keep Us Trapped — 99
Leaving It All Behind 99

    The Internal Experience Of Going No Contact 101
    Beware of Euphoric Recall 102
    Toxic Cycles 103
    Journal Prompt 110
    The Lessons Learned 110

8 Understanding Your Emotions   **113**
    A Lesson on Emotions 115
    Processing Emotions 121
    Feelings 122
    Recognizing Feelings Vs Emotions 123
    Journal Prompts 124
    The Lessons Learned 125

9 Triggers   **127**
    The Nervous System 128
    The Elevator Shaft 131
    What Is State-Shifting? 132
    Journal Prompts 141
    The Lessons Learned 142

10 Affect of Abandonment Fears   **145**
    About Fear 146
    Exploring Your Attachment Style 147
    Pushing Beyond the Fear 152
    Journal Prompts 157
    The Lessons Learned 158

11 Affect of Guilt   **161**
    Guilt Manifestations 163
    Recognizing Toxic Guilt Vs Healthy Guilt . . 164
    Toxic Empathy 165
    Toxic Empathy and Covert Narcissists 167
    Toxic Empathy and Enablers 167
    Toxic Empathy and Relationships Beyond
        the Narcissistic Parent 169
    The Benefit of Consequences 170
    Wiggle Your Toes. 172
    Using Anger Healthily to Kill Toxic-Guilt
        and Toxic Empathy 172

    Journal Prompts 173
    The Lessons Learned 174

12 Grief   177
    It's Ok Not to Be OK: Grief 177
    The Scapegoat's Grieving Journey 180
    The Stages of Grief 182
    Journal Prompts 183
    A Word of Comfort 184

13 The Things Beyond Your Control   187
    Letting the Cards Fall Where They May:
        Radical Acceptance 187
    What's Holding You Back? 189
    Empowered by Letting Go: Relinquishing
        Control 191
    Taking Back Control By Knowing Yourself . 194
    Questions to Help Identify Your Core Values 195
    Journal Prompts 197
    The Lessons Learned 198

14 Meet Your Shadow   199
    Becoming Aware of Our Programming 199
    The Shadow Self 201
    The Path of Shadow Work 203
    Steps to Integrate the Shadow Side Into Your
        Conscious Personality: 207
    Journal Prompts 208
    The Lessons Learned 209

15 Challenging Limiting Beliefs   211
    Limiting Beliefs 212
    The Scapegoat's Common Limiting Beliefs . . 212
    Limiting Beliefs and Cognitive Distortions . . 213
    Changing the Narrative 214
    The Meaning of Failure for the Scapegoat . . 216
    Tips and Tricks To Vanquish Limiting Beliefs 217
    Journal Prompts 220
    The Lessons Learned 221

16 Honor Your Sacred Self   223

Your Sacred Space 224
Your Environmental Sacred Space 225
The Sanctum Within 227
Your Physical Sacred Space 229
Self-Soothing Techniques 230
Exercises That Are Commonly Recommended for Releasing Trauma 230
Journal Prompts 234
Lessons Learned 234

17 Finding Happiness   237
Meeting Your Own Needs Without Feeling Guilty About It 238
A Need Is Not to Be Confused with a Want . 242
Tending To Your Inner Child 242
Train Your Mind to Focus on Gratitude Instead of Shortcomings 244
Simplify Your Life 246
Random Acts of Kindness 246
Your Body Can Influence Your Mindset . . . 247
Strike Up a Friendly Conversation with a Random Person 248
Choosing Happiness Doesn't Equate With Selfishness 248
Journal Prompts 250
The Lessons Learned 250

18 Beyond What You Know   253
Trust The Hero's Journey 253
We Are All Made of Light and Shadow: Love Yourself As a Whole, Not a Half 254
Taking Back What Is Rightfully Ours 257

Chapter 1

A Glossary about Narcissistic Family Systems

> That didn't happen.
> And if it did, it wasn't that bad.
> And if it was, it's not a big deal.
> And if it is, it's not my fault.
> And if it was I didn't mean it.
> And if I did, you made me do it.
> *(author unknown)*

Confusion, isolation, self-doubt, anger, frustration, guilt, shame, betrayal, and fear—these are the common experiences of scapegoated children as they grow into adulthood, striving to comprehend a fractured family dynamic. The relentless blame and emotional turmoil leave them questioning their own reality, yearning for a love that seems perpetually out of reach. This constant state of emotional dissonance can make it difficult to distinguish between what is healthy and what is toxic outside of the family, leading them to wonder as they grow into adulthood, "Is there something wrong with me?"

It can be challenging to discern normality when things have always been the way they are, and when your body tells you one thing, but everyone else insists on another. This contradiction leaves many survivors feeling fragmented, especially when they seem to be the only ones questioning the normalized dysfunction that everyone else has adopted as a way of life.

To outsiders, the scapegoated child's behavior can seem like a puzzle – their reactions baffling, their choices perplexing. Little do they know that the scapegoat's defiance, often perceived as rebelliousness, might be a desperate attempt to preserve their own identity in the face of relentless control. Their isolation, confusion, high reactivity, and disconnection may stem from years of having been punished time and again for their individuality and unbreakable spirit.

What outsiders may not fully grasp is that the unfortunate child who refuses to conform or accept the family dysfunction becomes the designated scapegoat.

Healthy Vs. Narcissistic Families

The notion that "no family is without flaws" is often used to dismiss the serious realities of dysfunctional families. Families, like most things in life, exist on a spectrum of how well they function. While no family is perfect, there's a significant distinction between healthy and dysfunctional family dynamics.

Healthy parents possess a good sense of self-awareness and emotional attunement with their children. This allows them to make decisions guided by wisdom and a deep sense of responsibility, prioritizing their children's well-being. When faced with their child's behavioral challenges, they don't shy away from introspection. They actively seek the root cause—is it bullying, parental conflict, poor communication, or unmet needs?

Furthermore, healthy parents understand that navigating emotions is new terrain for a child. They use communication, teachings, and empathy to help their children navigate these scary emotions. By addressing these issues at their source, they become the child's safe space, safeguarding their emotional, physical, and psychological well-being.

Children, like impressionable sponges, readily absorb the behaviors and attitudes they observe in their caregivers. Healthy parents recognize this and strive to model healthy practices and coping mechanisms for navigating life's challenges. This doesn't mean perfection, but rather an effort to manage their own emotions and avoid burdening their children with adult problems.

Healthy families provide a safe space for exploration, self-expression, and learning from mistakes without judgment (and within reason of course). Children are encouraged to pursue their passions, develop their talents, and chase their dreams. In essence, mutual respect and empathy form the foundation of a healthy family. These qualities create a nurturing environment where children feel safe, supported, and empowered to reach their full potential.

Be assured, the hallmarks of a healthy family are genuine. Dismissing them as an illusion is a form of gaslighting. Dysfunctional families will often deny their dysfunction, leaving those who see it for what it is bewildered, confused, guilty and silenced.

Therefore, let's shed some light on the other end of the spectrum. Narcissistic families create a toxic blend of conditional love, control, invalidation, and emotional manipulation. At the helm of this chaotic symphony is typically an emotionally dysregulated, emotionally neglectful, and antagonistic caretaker or influential family member. This central figure will treat their own children as mere extensions of themselves, emotional outlets, trophies for display, or disposable emotional trashcans. If the family suffers from the misfortune of having two narcissistic parents, the triangular dynamics become even more daunting for the children.

In this type of dysfunctional environment, mistakes are deemed unforgivable, denial is rampant, accusations are constant, and any attempt at self-growth that deviates from the narcissist's "vision," unrealistic expectations, needs, and desires is demonized. This stifling atmosphere leads to a culture where everyone must walk on eggshells to avoid the narcissist's unpredictable emotional outbursts, and any expression of dissent or non-conformity is met with shaming, criticism, and, most significantly, the withholding of love.

Most family members in a narcissistic family system are compelled to navigate the tumultuous waters of the narcissist's tantrums to evade further conflict. This dynamic fosters a system centered around appeasing the unappeasable. Although this will be vociferously denied when confronted, the reality remains that only one person is permitted to freely express a full spectrum of emotions without facing consequences.

The narcissist's constant roller coasters of mood swings, harmful behaviors, loss of touch with reality, complete disregard for how their behavior affects other family members, unrealistic expectations, blame-shifting, and at times, never-ending victimhood narrative are often excused and rationalized to "keep the family peace." It is precisely because of the enablers' compliance that the wheel of the dysfunctional family system keeps on spinning.

A telltale sign of a narcissistic family upbringing is consistently skewed priorities, with a perpetual malcontent at the center of it all.

Recognizing a Narcissistic Personality

People with a narcissistic personality style tend to have an inflated sense of self-importance and an inaccurate perception of their abilities and qualities. They often see themselves as superior to others and, paradoxically, believe they are generous and empathetic humanitarians who are not appreciated enough. They may use their selective kindness, generous deeds, and even tragic life stories to manipulate those around them. This creates a confusing dynamic where their positive actions seem to negate their harmful behavior. However, the reality is that these acts are often self-serving and fail to acknowledge the impact of their toxicity and abuse, particularly on those closest to them, especially their children.

It's important to note that the expression of these traits can vary greatly. Narcissistic personality exists on a spectrum, with some exhibiting mild characteristics and others meeting the criteria for Narcissistic Personality Disorder (NPD).

Common narcissistic traits include:

Inflated Self-Importance and Grandiosity:

Narcissists often view themselves as superior to others, exaggerating their abilities, talents, and achievements. They may believe they are uniquely gifted or destined for greatness. This inflated sense of self-importance manifests in a constant need for admiration and recognition.

Lack of Empathy:

Contrary to their self-perception, narcissists struggle to understand and share the feelings of others. They may even exhibit "mirroring" behavior, mimicking emotions to appear empathetic, but true emotional connection is absent. This lack of empathy can manifest in various ways, from dismissing another's pain to actively enjoying another's misfortune.

Excessive Need for Admiration:

Narcissists crave constant praise and validation, often manipulating situations to secure it. They may become envious of others who receive recognition and may belittle others' achievements to feel superior.

Entitlement and Arrogance:

Narcissists believe they deserve special treatment and are exempt from rules that apply to others. They may feel entitled to favors, privileges, and the best of everything. This entitlement fuels an arrogant attitude, where they view others with disdain.

Superficial Relationships:

Narcissists prioritize outward appearances and status symbols over genuine connections. They may form relationships based on what others can offer them in terms of admiration or validation, rather than a deeper emotional connection.

Unstable Emotions and Hypersensitivity to Criticism:

While they project an image of confidence, narcissists have fragile egos and struggle to regulate their emotions. Any perceived slight or criticism can trigger feelings of rage, humiliation, or shame.

Exploitation and Manipulation:

Narcissists view others as tools to serve their needs and desires. They may manipulate situations or use guilt trips to get what they want from others, often leaving a trail of emotional damage in their wake.

The Subtypes of Narcissism

As I embarked further on my journey to comprehend narcissism and its implications in my life, I unearthed that although there isn't an official clinical diagnosis for distinct subtypes of narcissism, peer-reviewed studies have recognized certain types, while mental health experts have informally labeled and brought attention to others. This implies that the quantity of narcissistic subtypes remains fluid. Nonetheless, discernible patterns often surface, underscoring the complex and diverse spectrum of narcissistic conduct.

The Grandiose Narcissist

The grandiose narcissist places utmost importance on upholding a positive image and garnering admiration, often neglecting to cope with frustration effectively. When faced with adversity, they may readily resort to anger. To them, parenting is akin to a performance, where significant events and milestones steal the spotlight, while daily emotional connection and involvement take a backseat. They are the type of parent who shows up only for the celebratory occasions but remains absent when their child needs them the most. They may assign unpleasant parental responsibilities to the other parent and push their child to excel in areas that reflect positively on themselves, such as academics, sports, or music. However, if the child fails to meet expectations in these areas, the parent may withdraw emotionally, prioritizing their own quest for approval and validation over their child's well-being.

The Malignant Narcissist

Malignant narcissists employ various tactics for manipulation and control, often resorting to fear to assert dominance. They perceive the world as threatening and project their own behaviors onto others, aiming to cultivate an environment of compliance. Their conduct is marked by impulsivity, exploitation, manipulation, and deceit, often accompanied by feelings of paranoia and sadism. They prioritize their own pursuit of power and pleasure over the safety and well-being of others, demonstrating little regard for their welfare. This disregard can lead to both physical and emotional aggression, driven by their conviction that others intend to cause them harm.

Covert Vulnerable Narcissist

Covert narcissists can be difficult to identify, as they hide their narcissistic traits behind a facade of vulnerability, humility, and victimhood. They often present themselves as shy, sensitive, and unassuming, but in reality, they are chronic malcontents with a deep-seated need for admiration and attention. They may use manipulative tactics like playing the victim to get what they want and avoid accountability for their actions.

These types of narcissists can be especially damaging to children, as they may exploit their vulnerability to manipulate and control them. They may play on the child's sense of guilt or responsibility to make them feel responsible for the parent's well-being. They may also use the child as a source of narcissistic supply, seeking validation and attention through the child's servitude and devotion.

Communal Narcissist

This type of narcissist often appears selfless and compassionate, but in reality, they use their charitable actions to gain validation and praise from others. They may neglect their own children's needs in favor of helping others, leaving the children feeling neglected and unimportant. The children may also struggle with confusion and disappointment as they see their parent being praised for their charitable actions, but not receiving the same level of love and attention at home.

This type of narcissism creates a powerful disconnect between the parent's public image and their true self.

Somatic Narcissist

Somatic narcissism is where the individual is preoccupied with their physical appearance, health, and bodily sensations. They may engage in excessive exercise, grooming, and/or cosmetic procedures to maintain their physical appearance and attractiveness. They also use their physical appearance to gain attention, admiration, and validation from others. Somatic narcissists often have a sense of entitlement and expect others to cater to their physical needs and desires. They may also use sex as a means of asserting their power and control over others.

Cerebral Narcissist

Cerebral narcissism, also known as intellectual narcissism, is characterized by a grandiose sense of self-importance based on intellectual or academic achievements. People with cerebral narcissism often believe they are intellectually superior to others and may use their intellect as a way to manipulate and control others. They may also have a sense of entitlement, an exaggerated need for admiration, and a lack of empathy for others.

Sexual Narcissist

Sexual narcissism is a term used to describe a type of narcissism that revolves around the individual's sexuality and sexual experiences. People with sexual narcissism tend to use their sexuality as a means of gaining admiration, validation, and power over others. They may engage in sexual activities solely for their own gratification and pleasure, without regard for the needs or feelings of their partners. They may also use their sexual encounters as a way of boosting their self-esteem and self-worth, and may seek out multiple partners to validate their desirability. This type of narcissism can be harmful to others, as it often involves exploiting and objectifying others for personal gain.

Neglectful Narcissist

Neglectful narcissists are self-centered and indifferent to the needs of their children or partners. They only engage with others when it serves their own interests and view people as mere tools to be used for their own benefit. They have little interest in any form of nurturing and caring for those closest to them. They are often cold, distant, and detached, and are not present in their children's lives. This is the parent or spouse who just isn't there.

Self-Righteous Narcissist

The self-righteous narcissist believes themselves to be morally superior. They are focused on following rules and doing things in a precise, rigid manner rather than from the heart. They may hold high-status jobs or positions of authority and can be very judgmental and critical of others. They may also be inflexible in their thinking and lifestyle choices, and may criticize the choices of others. They can be stingy with money, even if they have plenty of it, and may only use it as a means of punishment if a family member needs help. This type of personality is often ritualistic and obsessed with details.

Spiritual Narcissist

A spiritual narcissist is a type of narcissist who uses their spiritual or religious beliefs to gain power, control, and admiration from others. They may present themselves as spiritually enlightened or advanced, and use their knowledge and practice to manipulate and exploit others. They may also use their spiritual beliefs as a shield to avoid criticism or accountability for their harmful actions, and may reject or demonize anyone who challenges their spiritual authority or beliefs.

Generational Cultural Narcissism

Generational cultural narcissism transcends individual traits; it's a multifaceted phenomenon deeply rooted in a society's social and historical backdrop. In societies starkly divided by social class, gender roles, or authoritarian governance, those in positions of power often uphold control by systematically devaluing and marginalizing others. Over time, this societal narcissism, with its entrenched sense of entitlement, infiltrates family dynamics.

This sets the stage for the cycle of generational narcissism. Families mirroring societal divisions may instill in their children a belief in their inherent superiority, often at the expense of those labeled as "inferior." This dynamic may designate a scapegoat, perhaps based on gender, birth order, or personality traits, who is constantly criticized for failing to uphold the family's inflated image, while showering another child, the golden child, with praise, embodying the family's idealized self.

Children's Family Roles

Narcissistic parents tend to assign children into three distinct roles. These roles can shift based on the relationship between the parent and the child, and may even differ between the two parents if there are two narcissistic individuals in the household.

1. Golden Child: This child is the parent's favorite and embodies their idealized image of perfection. The parent may live vicariously through the Golden Child, who experiences immense pressure to maintain the illusion of perfection.

2. Scapegoat Child: This child is viewed as inadequate and is used as a target for the parent's anger, frustration, and dysfunctions. The Scapegoat Child is often subject to excessive criticism, abuse, and is labeled as problematic.
3. Invisible/Lost Child: This child is ignored and their basic needs are neglected by the parent, who shows little interest or awareness of their existence.

In addition to the main roles, children in a dysfunctional narcissistic family may adopt different coping mechanisms. These can include:

4. The Truth Teller: A child who recognizes the reality of the family dynamic and may question the "normality" of their experiences.
5. The Hero/Responsible Child: Often the eldest, this child may become a perfectionist and strive for high levels of success in order to hide the dysfunction of their family from others.
6. The Caretaker/Peacemaker/Fixer Child: This child takes on the role of a caretaker and peacemaker, but at the expense of their own well-being.
7. The Mascot/Clown Child: Using humor as a defense mechanism, this child distracts from the pain within the household.
8. The Mini Me Child: This child may develop narcissistic traits themselves as a result of mimicking the parent's behavior.

The Enablers

If the narcissist is a locked door, the enablers are the key that opens it, and the foot that prevents the door from closing.

Many survivors of narcissistic abuse struggle to understand the reasons behind their continued suffering, often without realizing that a key contributor to the cycle of abuse lies in the actions and inactions of enablers.

Enablers, Are the Narcissist's Fixers

A narcissist's grip on power is not the product of any gift or skill they possess, but rather from their drive and fixation on manipulating those in their circle to get what they want. This web of control is the cornerstone of their kingdom, but just like any empire, it needs faithful servants to maintain their image, carry out their commands, and sing their praises. Without these loyal followers, their mask falls and their rule crumbles.

The presence of enablers is crucial for a narcissistic system to exist. Without them, the narcissist would be held accountable for their actions; there would be no more abuse, no more blame shifting, and no more normalization of harm.

However, enabling is not a simple matter of people making deals with the devil.

I deduced that it starts with some sort of attachment to a person, a belief, or a cause. Many of us may have fallen prey to enabling because of the existence of such an attachment, without even knowing it. Have you ever defended a close friend without taking the time to hear the perspective of the other person first? Most of us probably have done this at least a few times in our life.

Some of us may have once followed relationship advice given by a respected leader, such as a priest, therapist, or coach, even though it wasn't the best advice we could have followed. When we form an attachment, or admire a person, there is a natural element of trust at play. We don't always question the things that people tell us.

Enabling can also take quite dark and twisted turns. For instance, providing alcohol to an alcoholic to ease their pain or refusing to set consequences out of fear of upsetting them, are both forms of enabling. Here, toxic empathy, a concept we'll explore in more detail later, can be a major player. Toxic empathy can make it difficult to set boundaries and can cloud our judgment, causing us to ignore warning signs or avoid seeking the truth. These strong bonds, fueled by a misplaced sense of compassion, can ultimately hinder both the enabler and the person being enabled.

In a narcissistic family system, enablers are often family members or friends who have formed some sort of attachment to the narcissist, sometimes long before the family scapegoat was born. In the case of siblings, this could have happened if they were the selected favorite and have been manipulated to view the scapegoat's mistreatment as deserved due to their "bad character," so to speak.

While some enablers may have shown kindness to the scapegoat and not been the source of abuse, their attachment to the narcissist always affects their decision-making, which, at the end of the day, has devastating consequences for the narcissist's main target in the family.

As someone who was once the family scapegoat, I vividly recall moments when my father and I shared a close bond in the calm of solitude. Our conversations flowed effortlessly, and we never got into disagreements. We always got along so well when my mother wasn't in the same room. However, her presence would transform everything. The father I knew would vanish, replaced by a subservient figure.

It was devastating to see the man who had shown me such kindness and understanding when we were alone - the man whom I always valiantly defended as a child and teenager every time she spoke horribly of him, painting him as an absolute monster of a father - suddenly throw me under the bus in the presence of the narcissistic queen who crowned herself as the greatest empath you could ever meet on this earth. It became the norm for my father to prioritize keeping the "peace" and avoiding another tantrum from my mother, even if it meant sacrificing our bond and my emotional well-being. I was expected to go along with this dynamic and keep my mouth shut, as the cycle of abuse and dysfunction in our family carried on.

In a narcissistic family system, the ball is always thrown around and around. "Go see a therapist, get some pills, and come back when you feel better." These were the last words I ever heard my father say when I pleaded with him to see how sick she had made me. This dismissal was the final blow, a clear message that I was on my own. The cycle continued – my pleas ignored, her behavior unchecked, and me, the scapegoat, left to navigate the fallout alone.

Realizing that the kindness received from those involved in a narcissistic family system isn't rooted in genuine love, but rather aimed at preserving the dysfunctional family dynamic, can be a harsh realization. Enablers, ultimately, act out of loyalty for the narcissist, and everything they do is to maintain the status quo and avoid upsetting the delicate balance of the system. Perhaps they did love us in some way, but their attachment to the narcissist is unmatched.

How many times have we bonded with enablers, shared pleasant conversations, and even found an empathetic ear when the narcissist wasn't around? However, like obedient soldiers who snap to attention at their superior's arrival, enablers may change their stance and behavior when the narcissist is present. One moment, they may appear kind and understanding, but in the next, they may turn their back on the survivor to placate the narcissist's unpredictable emotional states and maintain their position in the narcissistic system.

Other types of enablers may commiserate with the family scapegoat about the toxic behavior of the narcissist, but when the scapegoat bravely shares their own harrowing stories, seeking support, these enablers suddenly silence them, either by swiftly shifting the subject or abruptly ending the conversation. These enablers, who are not the primary targets of the abuse may opt to disengage from the situation and avoid getting caught in the crossfire, leaving the scapegoat to deal with their struggles alone.

This enabling behavior perpetuates the cycle of trauma, trapping survivors in a vicious cycle of abuse and pain. It is the attachment and love for these enablers that serve as the glue, preventing survivors from healing and breaking free from the toxic dynamics that continue to circle in loops.

Survivors of narcissistic abuse must confront the fact that their beloved family members, the ones they hold dear, are actually a greater threat to their well-being than the narcissist. When a person realizes that a family member is abusive, leaving them is not as difficult as when the abuser is surrounded by people that the survivor loves, shielding them from the consequences of their actions. The role of enablers is to protect what they are attached to - in this case, the illusion of peace in a dysregulated household - at the expense of the scapegoated family member. If the scapegoat chooses to leave, they will have to do so alone.

Common Types of Enablers

- The Pollyanna Enabler focuses on the positive qualities of the narcissistic family member and disregards or minimizes their negative behavior, even when the family scapegoat is being unfairly targeted.

- The Co-dependent Enabler supports the narcissistic family member's behavior by providing emotional, psychological, or physical support, perpetuating their dependence.

- The Martyr Enabler sacrifices their own needs to meet the needs of the narcissistic family member, even at the cost of neglecting their own children's emotional needs.

- The Silent Enabler doesn't speak out against the narcissistic family member's behavior, goes along with it even when they're aware of the harm.

- The Satellite Enabler orbits around the narcissistic family member, like for example a family friend who visits occasionally, and supports the narcissist.

- The Co-narcissist Enabler has their own narcissistic traits and forms a codependent relationship with the narcissistic family member.

- The Outlaw Enabler defies the narcissistic family member when they are not around, but still enables their behavior through their silence or loyalty to the family.

- The People Pleaser Enabler always tries to please others, including the narcissistic family member, even when it means ignoring the mistreatment of the family scapegoat.

- The Mini-me Enabler strives to emulate the behavior and traits of the narcissistic family member.

- The Flying Monkey Enabler actively participates in the manipulation orchestrated by the narcissistic family member.

Narcissistic Supply

Narcissistic supply refers to the attention, admiration, and validation that a narcissist constantly seeks from their environment to appease their inner chaos. They are emotional and psychological vampires who feed off the energy and emotions of others. If they don't receive the admiration or validation they seek, they will try to extract it from their victims by exploiting their vulnerabilities through emotional manipulation to evoke strong emotions. The stronger the emotions evoked in their targets, the more relief the narcissist feels.

This behavior is cyclical, and the narcissist will do it regularly. By exploiting their victims' discomfort and vulnerabilities through their antagonism, they further reinforce their sense of power and control.

Examples of how a narcissist might act to get supply include:

- Playing the victim: The narcissist may play the victim in order to evoke sympathy and attention from others. For example, they might make exaggerated claims about the difficulties they are facing, or use self-pity as a way to manipulate others.

- Triangulation: The narcissist may create conflict between two people and then insert themselves into the middle as the "mediator". This allows them to feel powerful and in control as they manipulate the situation and receive attention from both parties.

- Gaslighting: The narcissist may manipulate others by denying reality, making false claims, or trying to discredit others in order to maintain control and power in the relationship.

- Drama and conflict: The narcissist may create drama or conflict in order to receive attention from others. For example, they might start arguments, provoke others, or engage in behaviors that are designed to cause a reaction.

- Playing the hero: The narcissist may present themselves as a hero in order to receive praise and admiration from others. They may exaggerate their accomplishments, take credit for the accomplishments of others, or manipulate situations so that they can be seen as the hero.

In all these cases, the goal is the same: to receive attention and validation from others. The more intense the emotions that are evoked, the greater the sense of power and control the narcissist feels, and the more narcissistic supply they receive.

Gaslighting

Gaslighting is a form of emotional and psychological manipulation in which a person or group makes another person doubt their own perception of reality or sanity. The gaslighter uses a variety of tactics to distort, manipulate, and undermine their victim's perceptions and sense of self, often leaving them feeling confused, anxious, and uncertain.

Gaslighting can take many forms, including:
- Denying the victim's experiences or memories.
- Dismissing the victim's emotions or feelings.
- Making the victim doubt their own judgment or sanity.
- Questioning the victim's perception of reality.
- Using lies or half-truths to manipulate the victim's understanding of a situation.
- Twisting facts or events to make the victim appear irrational or unstable.
- Blaming the victim for things that are not their fault.

The effects of gaslighting can be long-lasting and damaging, often leading to feelings of self-doubt, confusion, anxiety, and even depression. Victims of gaslighting may struggle to trust their own thoughts and feelings, and may feel isolated and alone. Gaslighting is a dangerous and manipulative tactic that is often employed by narcissists and their enablers to control the designated scapegoat.

Triangulation

Triangulation is a manipulative tactic used to diffuse tension or shift focus away from the manipulator's behavior. It involves bringing a third person or thing into a conflict or relationship. This third party could be anyone – a family member, friend, coworker, even a video, book, prayer, or pet.

In a typical scenario, the manipulator will talk to the third person about the victim or conflict in a negative light about the victim, minimizing their own role. This creates confusion and betrayal for the victim, feeling ganged up on or unheard.

Triangulation is effective because it fosters an "us vs. them" dynamic, isolating the victim and making them feel like the problem. It also shifts the focus from the manipulator's actions to the victim, who then feels pressured to defend themselves against false accusations.

While sometimes unintentional, triangulation, regardless of intent, can be a form of emotional abuse or control. It's harmful and can cause long-term damage to relationships if left unchecked.

In a narcissistic family dynamic, triangulation involves pitting family members against each other. For example, a narcissistic parent might badmouth the scapegoat to the golden child, exaggerating and distorting facts about fights they themselves instigate. This creates a triangular dynamic where the sibling berates the scapegoat for upsetting the parent, who then feigns victimhood.

The ultimate goal is to maintain control over the family narrative, discredit the scapegoat's perceptions, and safeguard their authority. It's a cruel cycle of division and domination, where the truth is distorted to fit the narcissist's twisted view of the world.

Here are some common ways a narcissistic parent might triangulate their scapegoated child:

- Favoritism and Competition: A narcissistic parent constantly compares their favorite child to the scapegoat, showering the favorite with praise for even minor achievements while dismissing the scapegoat's accomplishments with a shrug or a backhanded compliment. This creates a competition fueled by the parent's favoritism, driving wedges between the siblings.

- Confusion and Blame: A narcissistic parent tells his spouse and children different versions of the same story, twisting details and planting seeds of doubt. This web of deceit breeds confusion and mistrust, leaving the scapegoat feeling isolated and questioning their own perceptions. The narcissist then swoops in, accusing the scapegoat of causing the family tension.

- The Perpetual Victim: A narcissistic parent constantly plays the victim, claiming to be unfairly treated by the scapegoat. They use dramatic outbursts or guilt trips to manipulate other family members into taking their side, solidifying their position as the wronged party and ensuring the scapegoat remains the target.

- Isolation and Control: A narcissistic parent deliberately withholds important information from the scapegoat, leaving them feeling excluded and confused. The parent then uses this as an opportunity to criticize and blame the scapegoat for their lack of knowledge or involvement in family matters, further tightening their control.

- Public Humiliation: A narcissistic parent may shame and criticize the scapegoat in front of others, causing them to feel embarrassed and humiliated. They might then turn to other family members for comfort and validation, painting themselves as the supportive parent and reinforcing the scapegoat's role as the "problem child."

- Secrets and Manipulation: A narcissistic parent may use secrets and privileged information to manipulate and control the scapegoat. They might threaten to reveal embarrassing details or use them as leverage in conflicts, keeping the scapegoat fearful and compliant.

- Inconsistent Treatment: The narcissistic parent's inconsistent treatment of the scapegoat child can be incredibly confusing and invalidating. While the parent may belittle their accomplishments in private, they may brag about them in public, using the child's successes to bolster their own image. This leaves outsiders, who have only seen the parent praise the child, with a distorted view of the situation, potentially siding with the narcissist when the scapegoat reacts negatively.

When the Enablers Take Part in the Process of Triangulation

- An enabler may publicly align with the narcissistic parent in criticizing and belittling the scapegoat, while privately offering them comfort and support. This creates confusion and division within the family.

- An enabler may use guilt-tripping tactics to pressure the scapegoat into submitting to the demands of the narcissistic parent, such as by saying things like "It's just for the good of the family."

- An enabler may present themselves as a mediator in disputes between the scapegoat and the narcissistic parent, but in reality, they are siding with the latter and reinforcing their abusive behavior.

- An enabler may manipulate the emotions of the scapegoat by offering false hope or playing on their vulnerabilities, all while maintaining loyalty to the narcissistic parent.

- An enabler may use flattery and praise to win the favor of the narcissistic parent, while undermining the credibility and self-esteem of the scapegoat. They will belittle the scapegoat, and reinforce the scapegoat's inferior status in the family, to secure the narcissist's approval.

- An enabler may act as a spy for the narcissistic parent, reporting back on the actions and words of the scapegoat to remain in good standing with the narcissist.

Examples of triangulating phrases:
- Your siblings/cousins don't seem to have a problem with the narcissist.
- This is why someone you cared about left you. Nobody could ever love someone like you.
- This is why your distant family members don't want to get to know you.
- You don't understand what is really happening in the family.
- You always cause conflicts with other family members.
- Why can't you be more like your sibling/cousin?
- My coworkers have a crazy family too. It's normal. You're the one who is irrational.
- It's the culture.
- You're the reason our family gatherings are never enjoyable.
- I've heard complaints about your behavior from multiple family members.
- Why can't you handle criticism and drama like your sibling does?
- Why can't you just do what I do? They are crazy around me too.
- I don't think you're capable of being a functional member of our family.

Smear Campaigns

A smear campaign is a calculated and deliberate attempt to damage an individual's reputation and credibility. Narcissists, driven by their need to be perceived as infallible, will go to great lengths to preserve their image and suppress any information that could tarnish it. This includes discrediting those who they perceive as a threat to their image, particularly when the scapegoat decides to cut ties with the narcissist. Narcissists will often portray themselves as the victim, falsely accusing their child of terrible behavior, and falsely claiming to have done everything for them, in order to maintain control and manipulate the perceptions of others.

Emotional Incest

In cases of emotional incest, a parent may rely on their child for emotional support and comfort, instead of seeking help from other adults. This can happen in many ways, including:

- Sharing inappropriate details about their personal life: For instance, a father might confide in his teenage daughter about his sexual problems with his wife, or a mother might tell her son about her marital problems.

- Treating the child as a surrogate partner: In some cases, a parent may seek emotional intimacy with their child that is more appropriate for a romantic partner. This can involve sharing secrets or engaging in inappropriate physical contact, such as cuddling or sleeping in the same bed.

- Pressuring the child to meet their emotional needs: A parent might make their child feel guilty or responsible for their emotional well-being. For example, a mother might say to her son, "I don't know what I'd do without you. You're the only one who really understands me."

When a parent engages in emotional incest, it can put a heavy burden on the child and interfere with their normal development. The child may feel responsible for the parent's emotional well-being, which can lead to anxiety, depression, and other emotional problems. They may also struggle to form healthy relationships with peers and partners, since they have learned that emotional intimacy involves taking on adult responsibilities rather than just being a child.

Enmeshment

Enmeshment is a family dynamic in which there is a lack of clear boundaries and differentiation between family members. This can occur in many ways, including:

- Over-involvement in each other's lives: The parents may make all decisions for the family as a unit, rather than allowing each individual to have their own autonomy. For example, parents might insist that their adult children live at home and follow certain rules, even if the children are ready to move out and live independently.

- Sharing too much information: Family members may share excessive amounts of personal information, blurring boundaries between what's appropriate and inappropriate. For instance, a mother might expect her daughter to disclose intimate details about her sex life and may resort to shaming or guilt-tripping to coerce her into sharing private information. Additionally, such a parent might invade their child's privacy by snooping through their belongings, monitoring their social media activities, or intruding into their personal space without permission, such as entering their apartment without knocking or being invited.

- Emotional enmeshment: Some families experience emotional enmeshment, where boundaries are so blurred that individual decision-making becomes difficult to separate from collective decision-making. For example, even if an adult son is already married with children, he may feel compelled to seek his mother's approval before making any major decisions that concern his work, wife or kids. Similarly, a mother may become overly invested in her son's life choices and disregard the presence of that son's spouse, causing tension among family members and unwanted triangulation in the son's marriage.

Parentification

Parentification can occur in families where one or more adult members are unable to fulfill their caregiving roles and the child is expected to fulfill such a role. For example, a child or teen may be expected to take care of their younger siblings, prepare meals for the family, or provide the family with financial assistance. They may also be expected to mediate family fights, play the therapist and constantly soothe an emotionally dysregulated parent.

In addition to missing out on normal childhood experiences, parentified children can also develop a sense of guilt and shame if they feel like they are not doing enough to care for their family. They may struggle with feelings of inadequacy and may have difficulty forming healthy relationships with peers due to their heightened sense of responsibility.

Parentification can also have a significant impact on a child's development. For example, if they are expected to constantly soothe an emotionally dysregulated parent, they may not have the opportunity to engage in age-appropriate activities or receive the guidance and attention they need. This can result in stunted emotional and social development and difficulty forming healthy relationships later in life.

Furthermore, parentification can lead to role reversal where the child assumes the role of the caregiver, while the parent becomes emotionally dependent on them. This can be a form of emotional abuse and can create a sense of confusion for the child, who may not fully understand the dynamics of their relationship with their parent. It can also be difficult for the child to transition out of this role, even as they become an adult, and can lead to ongoing emotional and psychological difficulties.

Infantilizing

Narcissistic parents may use infantilizing tactics to maintain control over their child, create a dependency on the parent, and undermine the child's sense of self-worth.

Some common examples of infantilizing:

- Overprotection: The narcissistic parent may overly coddle their growing child, teen, or young adult, treating them as fragile and incapable of handling the world independently.

- Control: The narcissistic parent may impose their decisions upon their growing child, teen, or young adult without considering their input, disregarding their autonomy even when they are capable of making their own choices.

- Belittling: The narcissistic parent may use patronizing language or belittle their growing child, teen, or young adult's achievements, downplaying their successes and highlighting their failures.

- Infantilizing language: The narcissistic parent may address their growing child, teen, or young adult with infantilizing language such as baby talk or pet names, dismissing their maturity and individuality.

- Ignoring boundaries: The narcissistic parent may disregard the boundaries and personal space of their growing child, teen, or young adult, invading their privacy and denying them autonomy.

Cognitive Dissonance

Cognitive dissonance is the story that people tell themselves to avoid disrupting their original beliefs, even in the face of contradictory facts. When people have a strong attachment to a particular belief, they tend to cling to it, regardless of evidence to the contrary. To maintain their belief, they may try to rationalize, find explanations, and make excuses, rather than questioning or revising their beliefs. This helps them hold onto their beliefs, despite contradicting evidence.

For example, the spouse of a narcissistic mother may experience cognitive dissonance when they witness the mother's abusive behavior towards the scapegoated child. They may struggle to reconcile the image of their partner as a loving and caring person with the reality of their partner's harmful actions. To ease this discomfort, the partner may try to justify the narcissist's behavior by blaming the child's adventurous temperament, making excuses for the narcissist's actions, or downplaying the severity of the abuse.

Cognitive dissonance can also play a role in the behavior of the narcissists themselves. They may justify their own abusive actions by believing that they are superior to others and therefore entitled to treat people poorly. They may also use cognitive dissonance to maintain their false image of themselves as a kind and generous person, despite their harmful behavior.

In both cases, the person is seeking to reduce their discomfort by aligning their thoughts and actions with their beliefs, even if those beliefs are distorted or harmful. It is important to recognize and address cognitive dissonance in order to break free from toxic patterns of behavior.

How To Think of Your Situation As the Family Scapegoat

When the scapegoat considers going no contact with a narcissistic parent, they must factor in that they will be leaving the entire system that operates around enabling a narcissist.

In my experience, the sad truth is that there will be no introspection upon the scapegoat's departure. Instead, the narcissist will embark on a smear campaign, claiming victimhood and other falsehoods, all in the guise of maintaining the image of the martyr. Meanwhile, the roles within the narcissistic family system will be redistributed; the narcissist always needs someone to blame, and another will be selected as their new source of supply.

The family dysfunction will continue because for meaningful change to occur, each person must take accountability for normalizing the workings of an unhealthy household. This is something that is most likely not going to happen. When the scapegoat lays down the final boundary to protect themselves from further harm, the show will only go on without them.

Leaving a narcissistic family system can be a harrowing experience, as it means losing more than just one parent, but the entire family unit. This heightens the already unbearable pain of the victim and forces them on a difficult journey. Many survivors choose the path of no contact as a last resort for the sake of their emotional and mental well-being, but this leaves them to confront their trauma solo, with a heavy burden resting on their shoulders.

However, beyond the grief, there is also life.

It is normal and healthy to grieve in the aftermath of leaving the narcissistic family system. I can attest to the indescribable pain of leaving behind those I once held dear. The darkness and sadness of abandonment is like a bottomless pit. When the people who are supposed to protect you, your own blood family, abandon you for being too sick to continue a relationship which has caused you too much harm, and which is the very reason why you got sick in the first place, it is only unfair.

But at the end of the day, you cannot control how a person reacts to your limits or boundaries. Your limits have been reached, and that is it. Every human being on earth has limits, and this is normal. What is not normal is how people in dysfunctional families seem to feel that there is no such thing as a boundary or a limit unless it is their own.

It is an enabling, toxic, rampant and dysfunctional belief, that if they can handle the toxic behaviors of a dysregulated narcissistic family member, then everyone should do the same in the name of "love". But should one family member voice their pain, express that their limits have been breached, or worse, get sick from the dysfunction, it's only because "they didn't try hard enough", "are disloyal to the family", "are weak", "irrational" and must therefore be disowned for their transgressions.

This is what "love" is like in a narcissistic family system.

Now Here Is What a Sane and Healthy Person Has to Say to You Instead:

Families are homes built on a foundation of trust and love. A toxic family can never be a home, because the foundation doesn't exist. A good family will see your boundaries and move around them, a toxic family won't even realize they're there. (Authors Unknown)

As a human being, you are entitled to the same

rules of decency and dignity as everyone else. This means you have the right to peace, emotional safety, privacy, respect, and especially sanity. You also have the right to choose your relationships; this means that it is within your right to say no to unhealthy and unsafe people in your life. It is no one else's prerogative to decide who is safe or unsafe for you, but your own, and anyone who does not respect this is unsafe for you.

Limits are normal, and boundaries are healthy. Money or favors do not cancel out abuse.

Your trauma is not measured in a currency that can be bought off and cancelled out in exchange for other goods.

You have the right to dream and pursue goals that are your own. You have a right to get angry when someone hurts you. You have the right to prioritize your mental health and do not owe anyone a relationship.

These are your rights, not privileges, contrary to the false beliefs that a narcissistic family system may try to force upon you.

As a survivor, you possess a strength and resilience that is unmatched. It is now time to trust yourself and make every step forward centred around your wellbeing, peace, happiness, and safety. Step back and view the situation objectively to see the truth of what has been happening to you.

This journey towards healing has its challenges, but it is necessary. You deserve to live your life in a peaceful, safe, and validating environment. That is your right. Each small step towards self-care is a victory. Every time you bring your attention inward and ensure that your emotional, physical, and psychological health is prioritized, you win.

Chapter 2

Behind Closed Doors: Seeing No Evil, Hearing No Evil

A recurring theme during my upbringing and adulthood was quite consistent in my blood family: denial, disbelief, minimization and collective amnesia.

No one believed me, and even when they did witness something, within a matter of days, it was forgotten as if it never happened.

I was consistently hammered down by denial and disbelief—disbelief in the reality I endured with my mother when no one was home, disbelief that a "kind, selfless, empathic, and sensitive soul" like her could actually do the things she did and twist the narratives on such a deep and incomprehensible level. I'm not kidding when I tell you that she once timed herself fainting right when my father walked in because she suddenly decided that day that I was to address her as "ma'am," not "mom," something that was never taught to us when we were kids or teens. This suddenly imposed mind-reading expectation was sudden and out of the blue.

I was in the midst of a conversation with her about something inconsequential, when suddenly she turned to me and screamed, "How dare you address me with such insolence! I am 'ma'am' to you."

This was new. In my entire upbringing, I had never been asked to change how I addressed her. She was always mom. This was a sudden, unexpected, and baffling new issue that she had created seemingly out of thin air. She initiated a huge drama, accusing me of disrespecting her on purpose by not suddenly calling her "ma'am," on that particular day.

As she escalated the fight over my inability to read her mind, my dad arrived in the parking lot. As he opened the door to come in, she dropped down to the floor and pretended to faint. He immediately looked at me with anger, believing I had done something terrible to his wife... again.

I attempted to explain what had happened, but I couldn't even express it because it made no sense.

Of course, she soon "painfully" got up with my father's help, shedding crocodile tears and dramatizing that the fight I apparently caused made her faint out of agony.

The stress caused by this woman's consistent fictional fights, which she has been doing since I hit my pre-teen years, was truly taking a toll on my mental health. I attempted to explain the situation to my dad, my sibling, and my friends. How does one explain something so absurd? My friends laughed it off, offering reductive advice such as "why don't you just set boundaries?" My sibling, as usual, didn't even register what I was saying. My father eventually stated that "she does have a point" and attributed the conflict to my supposed bad character. "Both of you have issues," he would say.

And despite everyone's inability to fully grasp what this woman was doing, my reality remained that I once stood over a woman who had apparently fainted because I did not address her as "ma'am." out of the blue. This was deemed inconsequential in my family.

In the aftermath, I had to deal with familial tension and blame for weeks, as she continued to play martyr and as usual reverted to the silent treatment. During this time, she would spin stories to my entire family about love, care, betrayal, and heartbreak at having such an ungrateful and demonic child. What did she do to deserve this? My supposed bad character was targeted and honed in on, and I was given speeches for my inability to just "do as they all did, and keep things cool with her".

As time passed and my dad once again spoke of peace and family love, luring me back in with another "happy" family gathering, I witnessed my sibling speak normally, addressing her as "mom," never once addressing her as "ma'am." Nobody, not even my dad, disagreed or said a damn thing about it. The conversations just went on and on and on. "Mom, mom, mom, mom..." No one said a goddamn thing.

Many people envision a flamboyant egomaniac when they think of a narcissist. However, covert narcissistic abuse manifests in more subtle ways, making it even more damaging for unsuspecting victims.

Covert narcissists don't rely on overt displays of arrogance. Instead, they weave a web of manipulation through subtle tactics like psychological manipulation, passive-aggressive behavior, and playing the victim. They will turn the people whom you love against you and ensure that you are bullied while they watch, feigning victimhood to garner attention and supply. Through personal experience, I have come to understand that this gives them a high, akin to drug addiction.

They excel at hiding their true nature. They can adeptly mirror other people, build trust and appear like wonderful souls. However, this facade masks a chronic malcontent who thrives on manipulating situations to elicit pity and shift blame.

These manipulators distort reality to appear

wronged, even if they instigated the conflict. They weaponize victimhood to evade accountability and justify their boundary-crossing behavior under the guise of self-defense, love or concern.

Deflecting Responsibility: The Martyr Syndrome

The term "DARVO" was coined by Jennifer Freyd, a psychologist and researcher in the field of interpersonal violence. The DARVO method is a common strategy used by perpetrators of abuse to deflect responsibility and avoid accountability. It is a pattern that often goes as follows:

- Deny: The perpetrator denies the accusation or wrongdoing outright, refusing to accept any responsibility.

- Attack: Next, they may attack the person making the claim. This attack could be in the form of blaming, shaming, or even accusing the victim of wrongdoing themselves.

- Reverse Victim and Offender: Finally, they may reverse the roles, portraying themselves as the victim and the actual victim as the offender. They may claim to be unfairly targeted or mistreated, deflecting attention away from their own actions.

My mother's patterns fit this model perfectly.

She would frequently seek me out to unleash her pent-up frustrations through fictional conflicts, sometimes multiple times a day. This was facilitated by my heightened reactivity, a result of enduring constant attacks, and the pervasive label of bad character that defined me in my family. She would covertly target my vulnerabilities, for instance, exploiting a friendship breakup when I was a young girl, by initiating triggering conversations like, "I wonder how your friend is doing. She was a lovely girl. It's such a shame she left after getting to know you. I really liked her. It's too bad you didn't hide your true character better."

Her poisoned words would provoke a reaction from me, causing me to scream at her to "Stop it!" My reactive response would immediately warrant punishment. She would then label herself as the victim, saying things like, "I was only showing concern, and this is how she treats me!" to other family members. "That friend was right to leave you," she would say covertly when no one was watching. "You will die alone and no one will ever love you."

This fulfilled her need for narcissistic supply, and shortly after the silent treatment ended, the cycle would begin again. The silent treatment could last for days, weeks, and even months once I reached adulthood. Had it not been for the flying monkeys who continued to dance to her tune, her silent treatments would have been a relief, as they signaled a time where I would be spared from invented conflicts and fictional fights. However, because of the presence of enablers, this peace never lasted very long.

My mother's behavior was enabled by the only family I knew, and despite my repeated attempts to communicate, reach out, and cry for help, the cycle persisted. I was consistently told that my inability to remain composed and "ignore her" was my own deficiency. I was always the one who was told to change.

In my family, it was deemed irrational and abnormal for a young girl to cry about the lack of normality, motherly love, and guidance in her life.

The Masks They Wear

A covert narcissist is skilled at shapeshifting and can adeptly wear different masks for different people and situations. They may have a mask for the outside world, a mask for their spouse, a mask for their favorite child, a mask for the scapegoat, and a mask for distant relatives and family friends. Their ultimate goal is always to manipulate others into perceiving them in a specific way, regardless of whether or not it aligns with their true character.

Narcissists tend to project a friendly and charming demeanor to those they deem non-threatening to their self-image. However, their true nature is only revealed to those who develop a closer relationship with them. This sudden shift in behavior can be highly confusing and disorienting. They can quickly switch from being charming to badmouthing family friends as soon as they leave the house, making racist, homophobic, and misogynistic comments, pulling out the superior-inferior cards, and becoming extremely judgmental. They may criticize their children's spouses, their children's children, release their frustrations onto those closest to them, hold grudges, withhold love, punish with silent treatments or physical violence, and exhibit a whole range of other toxic behaviors.

What's that? Someone is knocking at the door? At the slightest hint of an audience or interruption, their demeanor changes like a switch has been flipped. As soon as the doorbell rings or someone enters the room, they morph into the happy and loving parent, hiding any trace of negativity or hostility behind a facade of warmth and congeniality. This display underscores the chameleon-like nature of narcissists, who effortlessly switch between roles and personas to manipulate the situation and appease their audience.

After having carefully crafted the perfect image in public, it becomes too easy for the narcissistic parent to claim victimhood when the child who grows up, has reached their limits and no longer wants a relationship with them.

In a narcissistic family system, the victim is left to bear the burden of abuse alone when no one recognizes the true nature of the narcissist. The victim is often unjustly blamed not just by their own family, but also by the wider world, which is deceived by the mask that the narcissist puts on in public.

The trauma of a toxic relationship truly takes its toll when the scapegoat, who has endured all the abuse at home, is labeled as the "bad guy." The true victims of this type of abuse often become completely isolated due to the narcissist's skillful use of masks. Moreover, explaining the insidious nature of covert narcissism to those who haven't experienced it can be draining. To outsiders, it may seem like just one drop of water, and they may encourage the scapegoat to simply "get over it." However, they fail to grasp that this one drop has been falling in the same spot, steadily eroding away at the person's sense of self-worth, leaving a deep and lasting scar that only grows worse with time.

Beneath the Mask of Worry: Covert Manipulation Tactics

Covert vulnerable narcissists are masters of disguise. They cloak their manipulative behavior in a facade of concern, exploiting your empathy, love and need to be loved.

- Emotional Blackmail: They threaten to withdraw affection or even harm themselves if you don't bend to their will. "After all I've done for you..."

- Weaponized Worry: They twist situations to appear perpetually worried about you, justifying intrusive behavior and boundary violations. "I can't sleep at night knowing you're out with friends!" However, genuine empathy is absent, especially when you need support.

- Martyrdom and Guilt Trips: They exaggerate their sacrifices and paint themselves as the long-suffering caregiver. "Look at everything I've given up for you!" This guilt-tripping tactic keeps you obligated and focused on their needs.

- Isolating the Target: They subtly discourage you from seeking help or spending time with loved ones, ensuring you rely solely on them. "They don't understand you like I do." This isolates you and makes you more vulnerable.

- Controlling Through "Care": They may offer assistance with tasks, but their care comes with strings attached. They use this assistance to control the situation and make you feel indebted. Refusing their help often results in guilt trips, leaving you unable to say no without feeling guilty, and making you feel indebted for saying yes.

- Financial Control: Financial control is often disguised as "looking after your best interests." "You can't handle money; let me take care of it."

- Distorting Reality: They twist narratives to make themselves appear blameless and you the villain. "You're making me suffer with your ingratitude! I already suffered so much in my life!"

Journal Prompts

- Reflect on a recent interaction where you felt manipulated. Describe the situation and the specific tactics used.
- What are some of the things you were discouraged from saying or expressing in the relationship? Write a letter to yourself expressing those thoughts and feelings freely.
- Consider times you were made to feel guilty. What were the situations? Was the guilt justified? How can you challenge the guilt narrative?
- What are healthy boundaries you need to establish for yourself moving forward? How can you communicate these boundaries effectively?

- Reflect on your journey of healing. List all the ways you have grown stronger and more resilient as a result of this experience.

The Lessons Learned

Remember on your darkest days that the narcissist's behavior towards you is not a reflection of your worth as a person. Their actions stem from their own internal misery, and it is not your responsibility to fix or tolerate their toxic behavior. You don't owe them a relationship. The foundation of any healthy relationship is love and mutual respect, not worship, manipulation and emotional abuse when orders aren't followed.

By removing yourself from this toxic dynamic, you are prioritizing your own well-being and taking control of your life. It may be difficult to let go of relationships with enablers who have fallen for the narcissist's manipulation, but it is important to recognize that healthy relationships do not end because a third party threw yet another tantrum. If others choose to enable the narcissist and believe their false narrative, it is not a reflection of your worth or the validity of your experiences. Instead, it is a reflection of their own deep seated issues, lack of courage, poor values, and absence of integrity.

As you move forward on your journey towards healing and inner peace, it's likely that the narcissist and their enablers will persist in their destructive patterns. The enablers will continue to support the narcissist's behavior, sacrificing their own well-being for the illusion of "peace," while the narcissist will remain trapped in a cycle of victimhood and blame, perpetuating their own misery.

I invite you to recognize that this path is not conducive to healthy authentic living or peace.

While you cannot control the choices of others, you can have control over your own decisions. Prioritizing your well-being and happiness isn't selfish; it's a necessary act of self-care. This is your life, this is my life, this is every scapegoat's life, and I refuse to spend the rest of mine serving a chronic malcontent and their obedient servants, all under the pretense of it being done in the name of love. This is a lie. Let me assure you that none of this has anything to do with love; rather, it's about power and control.

Some key points to remember:

When meeting new people, be cautious of those showering you with immediate affection, favors, or excessive concern. This intense "love bombing" can be a tactic to gain control. Also, be mindful that healthy relationships develop gradually. Trust your gut if something feels off. Don't feel obligated to accept "freebies" that create an uneven power dynamic.

Remember, genuine kindness doesn't come with hidden expectations. Be wary of those who use acts of kindness to guilt you into loyalty or manipulate you later.

Finally, not everyone who appears vulnerable truly desires help. For some, the victim role becomes a comfort zone or even an addiction. They derive satisfaction from the attention they receive by playing the victim, as it becomes a stable source of supply for them. This behavior allows them to avoid responsibility and accountability for their lives and serves as a convenient way to deflect any wrongdoing onto others, keeping their image perfectly clean.

These types of people find comfort in maintaining and preserving the victimhood role, claiming illnesses, portraying themselves as victims of circumstance, and using their life stories as justification for hurting others. They may expect others to read their minds, serve them, walk on eggshells around them, and inflict punishments and silent treatments when their expectations aren't met, all while neglecting to acknowledge the suffering and pain their behavior may cause to others who genuinely care for them, or to those dependent on them, such as their children.

Be warned that when confronted with people who

genuinely struggle, and with whom they have nothing to gain from, such as someone who falls ill or faces adversity, not only will their pain be dismissed as mere theatrics, receiving little to no empathy if it disrupts the narcissist's life, but it will also be viewed as competition. Everything revolves around the narcissist's perspective: How will this affect their life? Will it disrupt their supply? Will it cause inconvenience?

Remember, as long as you continue to pick up their broken pieces, they will continue breaking more pieces.

...and accuse you of forcing them to break the pieces while they are at it.

Chapter 3

Conditional vs Unconditional Love

The "Love" Experience for the Family Scapegoat

The word "love" is often wielded by narcissistic parents as a means to "make everything better" when it isn't. It becomes a tool for suppressing the victim's emotions and experiences, conditioning them to accept unhealthy and dysregulated behavior as part of the "deal" of having love in one's life. Suddenly, the same person who has repeatedly inflicted harm on the victim, or the enabler who stood by and did nothing, such as the other parent, utters the word "love" to trigger the victim's toxic empathy, shame, false responsibility, and guilt, like flipping a switch.

But they love you...yeah?

It's as if the scapegoat is expected to suddenly think, "You love me? Oh, gosh, my bad! I apologize for hurting you by being hurt by you. I am so sorry for having boundaries. You're right, we're family, so I should sacrifice my emotional safety and mental health in the name of love. You continue to hurt me because you are a victim. You are right, I am unreasonable, and the ball is entirely in my court now. My bad! Let me try to put myself together once again real quick, so that I may return to the cycles of this relationship. Oof! You say you love me! That changes everything. I feel so much better! Let me pack my bag, come home and hope for the best!"

In reality, the word "love" is a twisted form of control, meant to manipulate the victim into accepting abuse and neglect.

Through my highschool years, I found myself slowly self-destructing. It was a downward spiral, seeking solace among other teens, cigarettes, alcohol, and cannabis, my future directionless, my priorities confused, my mother's words echoing in my mind, becoming a self-fulfilling prophecy. I did everything to escape her, from couch surfing to moving out long before I was ready.

As I entered college, I struggled to make ends meet. I was going to school full time, and worked full time with very little financial assistance from my family, as no college fund was ever set aside for me of any kind. Seeing me struggle, my father would encourage me to come back, reassuring me of safety, a loving home, and a waiting bedroom. Sometimes, during these luring-back periods, my mother would suddenly be on speaking terms with me again as well, creating a fantasy version of what life would be like at home, where I could study peacefully and not worry so much about money. It was difficult not to fall for the fantasy version of life she painted for me, as I was still in many ways a child and in dire need of guidance and belonging.

I desperately wanted to believe that these words would hold true. And so, I would go back to that house, after my perceived "failed" attempts in adulting. But as soon as I found myself under her roof, the dysfunction resumed, and intensified, as if I never left. And, of course, when I tried to voice my distress at her escalating conflicts and daily antagonisms, I was painted as ungrateful for all the wonderful things I have been given. All in all, college led me to burn out, and my mental health only deteriorated further.

There was nowhere to go and no one to turn to. My sibling, who had already been out of that house for a few years, and who blocked any memory of our childhood and teen years, had a habit of laughing hysterically when I would reach out to him, claiming that "Her behavior was so funny!" My father would simply repeat, "Your character is not perfect either." Beyond those two family members, there was no one else to reach out to as I had never gotten to know my family abroad. Moreover, my mother demonized me in her phone calls to them, portraying me as a horrible child who consistently made her suffer, whenever she had the chance. I could hear everything from my room, every time she did it, since my young years. As a result, I avoided getting to know them out of fear of more bullying.

Sometimes, the gaslighting got to me, and I thought to myself that maybe I truly was guilty and flawed, and maybe I needed to try harder. After all, I was reactive, and I couldn't understand why.

Maybe they where right about me and I needed to try again?

So, I tried to be nice, I tried to stay silent, I tried to communicate my feelings constructively, I tried to tiptoe and tiptoe and tiptoe. Nothing ever worked, and the only thing that I have deduced from this is that in a narcissistic relationship, anything you do or say will be used against you one way or another in the narcissistic court of law.

Once they have a fixation on you, you become the target of all the hatred, loathing, frustrations, and evil they carry within, and there is nothing you can do to change this.

When Love Is a Poisoned Apple

Love is a complex concept for scapegoats, particularly in narcissistic family systems where it is often used in a different manner than in healthy families. It's reminiscent of the tale of Snow White, who innocently bites into an apple presented by an old lady in the guise of kindness and care. Similarly, scapegoats may find themselves drawn to the illusion of love and acceptance, only to realize later that it was a toxic trap.

Healthy and genuine love is a profound and all-encompassing emotion, demonstrated through actions and behaviors that show care, respect, and consideration for others. In healthy relationships, mutual respect is paramount, and people do not consistently belittle or devalue each other. This behavior is not "normal" as the narcissistic family system will have their scapegoat believe.

Narcissists, consumed by their obsession with power and control, view relationships as battlegrounds where they must emerge as winners, dominating and conquering others. This warped perspective leads to toxic dynamics where empathy, compassion, and genuine connection are replaced by manipulation, exploitation, and emotional abuse.

For a narcissist, love must be unconditional in one direction, while being conditional in the other.

Conditional Love Vs. Unconditional Love

Conditional love is a type of love that is contingent upon certain conditions or behaviors being met. In other words, the love and acceptance a person receives is dependent on them meeting certain expectations or standards. This type of love is often characterized by manipulation, control, and demands for compliance. It can be unpredictable and can be withdrawn or given based on the actions of the other person.

Unconditional love, on the other hand, is a type of love that is not dependent on any conditions or behaviors. It is a love that is given freely, without any expectations or demands. It is characterized by acceptance, understanding, and support. It is constant and stable, and is not affected by the imperfections of the other person. It is a form of love that values the person for who they are as a whole and accepts them without reservation.

While it is normal in any relationship to have a degree of expectations, such as mutual respect and collaboration, a narcissist takes expectations to a whole new level. Their expectations revolve around controlling, overpowering, and manipulating others.

This is how they twist and distort the narrative of love. It is my firm belief that for the scapegoat dealing with this, there is little that can be done to change the dynamics of the relationship unless they go no or low contact to protect themselves. It is a mindset, a mentality, and a complete lack of introspection that isn't within the scapegoat's power to change.

Unconditional Love Feels Like:

- Safe Haven: You feel completely accepted for who you are, flaws and all. It's a safe space to be yourself without fear of judgment.

- Empowerment: You're encouraged to grow, and learn from your mistakes. Your unique qualities and individuality are celebrated.

- Mutual Respect: Your feelings, thoughts, and decisions are valued, even if they differ from the other person. Boundaries are respected, fostering trust and security.

- Supportive Presence: They're there for you through thick and thin, offering a listening ear and unwavering support. They celebrate your successes, big and small, with genuine joy.

- Healthy Communication: Communication is open and honest, even during disagreements. Issues are addressed constructively with empathy and a willingness to understand each other's perspectives.

Conditional Love Feels Like:

- Walking on Eggshells: You constantly feel like you need to be on guard, worried about saying or doing the wrong thing and losing their affection.

- Manipulation: Love feels like a tool used to control your behavior or emotions. Guilt, shame, or obligation are used to keep you in line.

- Emotional Rollercoaster: The amount of love and affection you receive fluctuates based on their needs or whims, leaving you feeling insecure and confused.

- Comparison Trap: You're constantly compared to others, making you feel inadequate and like you can never measure up.

- Heavy Burden: The relationship feels draining and one-sided. You feel responsible for their happiness, and their negativity weighs you down.

Safe Vs Unsafe People

When one evaluates the safety of a relationship, it is important to remember that everyone messes up sometimes. Occasionally messing up doesn't necessarily make a person unsafe. Paying attention to a person's recurring patterns will help you make the distinction between making an honest mistake, and being unsafe.

Because people don't often show their true colors right away, a person who once felt safe, may become unsafe after some time. Also, be aware that a person who is safe for you, may not necessarily be safe for someone else, and a person who is safe for someone else, may not necessarily be safe for you. This is why you should rely on your feelings, your senses, and your wisdom when making such a decision.

Unsafe Person Signs

- Prioritizes rules, laws, religion, and perfectionism over your needs and feelings.
- Believes they are always right and above reproach.
- Uses toxic positivity as a way to dismiss or minimize your valid concerns or negative emotions.
- Engages in excessive flattery to manipulate and win your favor. Guilt-trips you.
- Creates confusion by sending mixed signals or contradicting themselves.
- Believes they always know more than you, regardless of the subject matter.
- Pressures you into having or maintaining unhealthy relationships with people they choose.
- Demands trust without earning it or being trustworthy themselves.
- Interrogates, reacts, attacks based on assumptions rather than asking for clarification or seeking understanding.
- Uses inappropriate humor, mocks, belittles, or makes hurtful comments.
- Maintains a negative mindset and discourages.
- Engages in gossip or badmouths others, often without cause.
- Insists on having their way.
- Blames others for their mistakes or problems, never taking responsibility themselves.
- Is inconsistent; their treatment of you will depend on their mood or on their "thought of the

day".
- Engages in self-destructive behaviors.
- Makes inappropriate, passive-aggressive, or hurtful comments that undermine your self-esteem or well-being.
- Places themselves and others on a superior/inferior scale, making unfair comparisons or judgments.
- Holds others responsible for their own insecurities or emotional sensitivities.
- Betrays confidences and shares secrets that were meant to be kept private.
- Uses money or gifts to buy or manipulate love and affection.

Safe Person Signs

- Prioritizes your wellness above rigid rules, laws, religion, or perfectionism.
- Demonstrates humility.
- Respectful towards you and others.
- Consistently treats you with kindness and consideration.
- Respects your boundaries.
- Encourages you to spend time with loved ones and respects your social connections.
- Lifts you up.
- Is genuinely happy for you and others when good things happen.
- Is reliable and keeps their promises. You feel confident that you can depend on them.
- Is honest and transparent with you, even when it's hard.
- Maintains consistent behavior regardless of the presence of others.
- Practices self-care, takes responsibility for their own well-being.
- Is self-aware.
- Makes effort to manage difficult emotions, and is mindful of how they affect others.

- Recognizes when they are wrong and apologizes when appropriate.
- Asks for clarification or input when needed.
- Reaches out to you, just because they genuinely care.
- Values equality and shows it in their actions and behavior.
- Accepts you as you are.
- Is open to feedback and works towards personal growth and improvement.
- Speaks positively of the people close to them and avoids gossip.
- Demonstrates patience and understanding, even in difficult situations.
- Keeps your confidences and doesn't betray your trust.
- Shows love through thoughtful actions and gestures.

About Forgiveness

What do forgiveness, empathy and compassion have to do with one's own fundamental need for emotional safety in a relationship?

These concepts are distinct and should not be conflated.

Too often, the expectation for the scapegoat to forgive and forget persists, even in the absence of remorse, accountability, or any indication of change from the abusive parent. This is inherent in narcissism, where the abuser refuses to admit wrongdoing and justifies their actions without end.

The expectation to forgive a narcissistic parent often falls as yet another burden on the scapegoat, already weighed down by years of abuse and conditioned false responsibility for burdens that were never theirs to bear in the first place. "They had their own trauma," well-meaning voices chime in, urging reconciliation for the sake of having "one parent left."

But what a scapegoat truly needs is validation and healing, not forced forgiveness, or shaming if this is something that they simply cannot do. Our pain is genuine, our experiences real, and our boundaries and limits deserve to be respected. We need to be freed from the endless cycle of discussing the narcissist's past and emotions—a narrative that has consistently been used to deflect attention from every single incident of physical, emotional, and psychological abuse many of us have endured over a lifetime.

This constant focus on the narcissist's "hurt" becomes a weapon, further targeting the already targeted scapegoat. True healing requires escaping this very dynamic and prioritizing our well-being, needs, and limits—something that we have never been given permission to do in our own families.

Furthermore, genuine forgiveness isn't about erasing memories; those remain indelible. Instead, it involves releasing the hatred and resentment within oneself for one's own well-being and healing. However, when therapists or other people insist that the scapegoat forgives their abusers due to their troubled lives or their personality disorder, they also seem to insist that forgiveness must come with the expectation of mending a relationship that does not change and remains abusive.

It's essential to clarify that forgiveness doesn't obligate anyone to maintain a relationship with those who persist in displaying abusive behaviors. If the cycle of abuse continues, each person has their own agency to forgive, or not, and part ways.

Sure, we can empathize with someone by understanding their challenging past and granting them forgiveness. Yet, when they continuously use their past as a justification to hurt their own children, feeling entitled to harm someone vulnerable and "beneath them" in the hierarchy of the system because they themselves feel hurt, then the scapegoat becomes condemned to living in chains. They are robbed of their right to peaceful living. They are robbed of their right to safety. They are robbed of their right to freedom.

A narcissist understands the difference between right and wrong. They can wear masks of love and empathy to gain admiration and sympathy when it suits them, but they also know when to discard those masks. They understand which cards to play and when to play them to be liked, and they are perfectly aware of the difference between good and bad. They are masters at crafting the image they want to preserve for the sake of being admired, liked, and loved. Unfortunately, malevolence is real, even though the world may not be ready to hear it.

Too often, discussions about forgiveness portray the abuser as the only victim, sidelining the actual victim and compelling them to persist in a traumatic relationship where the dynamics simply do not change.

Forgiveness doesn't imply maintaining a toxic, unchanging relationship. There comes a point where genuine empathy transforms into harmful toxic empathy, enabling the abuser, which is essentially how the entire narcissistic family system operates in the first place.

Genuine forgiveness entails releasing resentment and letting go. However, it does not necessitate maintaining a harmful or toxic relationship. This decision is deeply personal and should be made without external pressure or judgment.

Let's not confuse forgiveness with enabling or tolerating harmful behavior. True forgiveness empowers us to free ourselves, but does not take away our agency to set boundaries, and select who we welcome into our lives.

Journal Prompts

- Consider the conditions you place on yourself in order to feel deserving of love and acceptance. Are these conditions realistic or fair? How do they impact your self-esteem and relationships?
- Consider the balance between setting healthy

boundaries and offering unconditional love. How can you honor your own needs and boundaries while still fostering love and connection with others?
- Reflect on any insights or revelations that arise from exploring the concepts of conditional and unconditional love. How can you apply these insights to cultivate more fulfilling and authentic relationships in your life?
- Write a letter to yourself exploring what it would mean to fully embrace unconditional love in your life. What changes might you need to make, and how would it impact your relationships and overall well-being?

The Lessons Learned

Growing up scapegoated meant that love was dangled in front of you like a carrot on a stick, given and withdrawn cyclically. A narcissistic parent held the strings, only lavishing affection and validation upon you when you met their demands, whether it be excelling in school, dressing like a perfect little doll, keeping quiet about your true feelings, tending to their emotional needs, or completing household chores. This type of love was based on performance, behavior, and achievement, conditioning you to believe that you were only deserving of love if you met certain requirements.

As you ventured out into the world, seeking love and acceptance, you may have found yourself drawn to those who mirrored this conditional love. The past has a way of repeating itself, and the pain of your childhood may have unconsciously led you to seek validation from those who were similarly demanding and never satisfied.

And so, as you embark on a journey of self-discovery, self-compassion, and self-acceptance, I invite you to change this narrative and halt these cycles from repeating themselves in endless loops.

Learning to give oneself unconditional love requires prioritizing oneself, validating oneself, believing in oneself, and protecting oneself—tasks that may feel foreign at first.

Unconditional love is not something that we are born with; it's something that we learn and cultivate over time. We begin by understanding that we don't need to be perfect to deserve respect, that mistakes are a part of the human experience, and that our flaws do not justify mistreatment. Self-compassion teaches us to let go of the need for perfection and instead approach self-improvement with curiosity and openness.

You can gradually learn to be your own source of validation and acceptance, rather than seeking it outside, by tapping into your own felt sense and paying attention to what your body needs. It's a journey that requires patience and practice, but by committing to it, you can learn to love and accept yourself, exactly as you are right now, without changing a goddamn thing.

Chapter 4

Gaslighting

"It Never Happened"

> "The greatest trick the Devil ever pulled was convincing the world he didn't exist."
> *The Usual Suspects (1995)*

I thought it was quite fitting to begin with a quote that encapsulates the insidious nature of gaslighting in a narcissistic family system so perfectly. Just as the devil in the quote convinces the world of his non-existence, the narcissist and the enablers convince the world, and even themselves, that the dysfunction poisoning their household doesn't exist.

And when one fights back against something that doesn't exist, they can only be labelled as crazy.

I recall a specific event, one of many, that exemplifies the gaslighting that I have been subjected to within my narcissistic family dynamic.

I broke my leg. I slipped on wet grass while walking a dog. During this period of my life, I had just given birth to my second child, while the first had begun his toddler stage.

After leaving the hospital, my husband and I felt overwhelmed with the prospect of managing our parental responsibilities with me being confined to bed, especially since he had no relatives in the country, and my own extended family resided abroad. My sibling had his own family and children to care for, and so with no one else to turn to for help, we decided to bypass returning home after I was discharged from the hospital and headed straight to my parents' house, seeking my father's support. In the car, I sat with my leg elevated, sandwiched between two babies secured in their car seats.

I felt an overwhelming sense of anxiety, knowing that I would struggle to care for my children alone since I couldn't move or bend without help.

That visit proved to be futile.

The moment I entered their house, my mother chose to paint my distress as a personal attack. The focus shifted towards her victimhood and the burdens that I allegedly always brought to my family. The entire conversation was twisted around my character, my tone of voice, my facial expression, and my perceived angry attitude problem, as usual.

There was nothing that I could do. Any emotion on my part that wasn't joyful made my mother "suffer", and I struggled to maintain my composure. So, I confronted her lack of empathy, exclaiming, "Really? You honestly think that my distress is a burden to you right now? But it was too late; after reacting to her narrative, the ball was in my court.

I was the bad guy once again.

Of course, my father, being the good enabler that he was, only stood there and did nothing, as he usually did when she was there.

Needless to say that I quietly cried for the entire ride back, lying in the backseat, looking at my children and wondering how I was going to manage keeping them happy and healthy with no family help.

As my husband managed to convince his boss to let him work from home for some time and somehow balanced work and caring for a toddler and a baby throughout his shift, I struggled to help. I could only cradle one baby in my arms without being able to prepare food or watch my toddler, who had entered his "terrible twos" phase.

And then, two weeks into my ordeal, I received a phone call from my father. However, instead of offering help or checking on the kids, he asked for a favor. My mother needed help giving their cat flea medication, and she didn't understand how to open the tube properly. To say I was upset is an understatement. No concern for me and their grandchildren? Flea medication for their cat?

A fight ensued, and I hung up the phone, absolutely triggered and shocked. That night, I received an angry email from my father, criticizing my attitude, dismissing the significance of a broken leg, claiming he had been through worse, and blaming my "attitude problem" on the fact that they hadn't come to help. No grandparents visited or checked on their grandchildren for the remainder of my recovery period. Nobody came to help. Ironically, when Christmas came around, small presents and cards were dropped off at the door... because that's what love is all about in my family. How ironic.

It took me months to be able to walk again without a cast, and although a few friends occasionally helped out, my husband and I had to manage on our own. A year later, my father resurfaced, and he hoovered me back into the family fold, as he always did, through his love. Eventually, I returned, because family forgives. Yeah?

This was what my therapist encouraged me to do as well.

At the time, I still saw my father as the good parent, a loving figure who was caught in the crossfire of a bad relationship and his love for his daughter. I felt bad for him. I felt like he was brainwashed by her and that he was suffering as much as I was. Through the lens of guilt, I didn't consider that he might have intentionally not come. I rationalized that he couldn't come because my mother manipulated him, and it wasn't his fault.

So I went back.

As the "happy" family gatherings resumed, on a fine evening, my mother brought up the subject of my broken leg in a nonchalant manner. "Remember that time you rejected my help when you broke your leg?" Everything about that statement, and her attitude around it, made me shake from the inside.

"We called you to offer help, and you rejected us," she continued. "Remember that phone call?"

To this day, her narrative stands. She had constructed a false narrative where she claimed to have repeatedly offered help, portraying me as her ungrateful and irrational daughter who rejected her aid.

My mother convinced herself, and anyone who listened to her, that I had rejected her help when I was absolutely desperate for assistance, with two babies under my care. My husband and I struggled terribly to maintain a level of normalcy for our young children while I was bedridden. And yet, here we are.

This specific event was the tipping point for me to try and understand what I was dealing with. I didn't know what gaslighting was, nor did I know how to research it. Narcissism wasn't an ongoing trend just yet during those years. I dove headfirst into research, devouring articles one after another until a truth slammed into me: narcissism. Every detail checked out. It was a horrifying moment of clarity, a confirmation of the manipulation I'd been experiencing.

That day, I learned that validation was never going to come through my blood relatives. It was going to come through education.

When Gaslighted, You May Experience:

- Feelings of Confusion.

- Ruminations about the relationship.

- You doubt your ability to reason.

- You feel guilty or responsible for things that are not your fault.

- You have a hard time making decisions or trusting your own judgment.

- You find yourself constantly apologizing.

- You feel isolated and alone, as if no one believes or understands your experiences.

- You feel like you are "walking on eggshells" around the other person, trying to avoid their anger or disapproval.

- You feel like you have to constantly "prove" your own reality to others.

Gaslighting is a form of emotional abuse, and enablers are equally responsible as the narcissist for perpetuating the toxic cycle within the family system. By failing to hold the narcissist accountable for their behavior, enablers prolong the abuse and directly contribute to keeping the victim trapped in the cycle of abuse.

In a narcissistic family system, gaslighting of the scapegoat is constant, becoming a way of life.

"But she worries about you," was the constant narrative from my family, followed by, "You're not perfect either, you know?" This refrain echoed after every single incident, without fail.

It's sickening to think that these narcissistic tendencies become normalized to the point where the narcissist is always seen as the compassionate winner, and the scapegoat is viewed as the ungrateful and evil loser. The scapegoat is always deemed as the perpetrator, even if they are the ones who are injured, traumatized and ostracized.

The Gaslighter's Toolkit

Gaslighters have a toolbox designed to distort reality and control the narrative.

Emotional Invalidation

Having your thoughts, feelings, and experiences dismissed or invalidated, making you feel unheard and questioning your own reality.

Memory Manipulation

Being told your memories or perceptions are wrong, causing confusion and self-doubt about your past experiences.

Isolation

Being pressured to cut off contact with friends, family, or support systems, or witnessing the people you love being manipulated by the narcissist to have a negative and distorted view of you, leaving you vulnerable and alone.

Minimizing Abuse

Being told toxic behavior is normal or you are overreacting, normalizing the abuse and making it difficult to identify.

Cultural Gaslighting

Being told the abuse is part of the family culture, making it seem like you are wrong to question it.

Planting Seeds of Doubt

Being made to feel like you are crazy, paranoid, or delusional, eroding your trust in your own judgment.

Shifting Blame

Being accused of causing the family member's bad behavior or blamed for the family's problems.

Conditional Love

Being told you are not loyal, grateful, or a "real" member of the family unless you act a certain way.

Silencing Opinions

Being told you cannot have your own opinions or that your opinions are insignificant in the "bigger picture".

Emotional Shaming

Being scoffed at or shamed for trying to express your feelings.

Gaslighting by Evidence

Being dismissed when you provide proof of your experiences, further manipulating your perception of reality.

Controlling Communication

Being told not to bring up family issues with outsiders or seek help as they will think that you are crazy.

Techniques to "un"gaslight Yourself

Boost Your Reality Awareness

You must become an active participant in validating and acknowledging your own reality. To do this, try this exercise in a private or quiet environment where you feel at ease. Start by speaking out loud and naming the actions and decisions you make throughout the day. Here are some examples:

- "I am taking a shower, I am using the shampoo, I am washing my hair."

- "I am making breakfast, I am frying an egg, I am toasting bread."

- "I am getting dressed, I am putting on a red shirt, I am choosing blue pants."

By speaking out loud, you're strengthening the validity of your actions and helping your brain make the connection between your experiences and the words you're using to describe them. This exercise can aid you in overcoming gaslighting and reinforce your sense of reality.

Ungaslight Yourself by Listening to Your Body

Your body is your ally. It knows about everything that has ever happened to you. It is the most important witness to the whole story of you. Trusting your body's messages is an important aspect of self-care and self-compassion. It allows you to connect with your inner self, to listen to your intuition, and to understand your emotions. Your body is a powerful tool, and it can help you navigate through life's challenges by providing you with signals and messages that can guide you towards taking care of yourself. These signals can be physical sensations such as pain, discomfort, or tightness, or they can be emotional sensations such as anxiety, sadness or anger. I would invite you to pay particular attention to disgust, as disgust is a warning sign of toxicity. Your body is telling you to stay away, as this person is poison.

The purpose of these messages is not to hurt you but to communicate important needs. Get curious about what your body is telling you, and strive to understand what it needs from you and where it needs attention and healing. By listening to our emotions and paying attention to what our body is telling us, we can gain valuable insights into our needs.

Acknowledge the Ridiculousness of It All

Honestly, if you allow yourself to take a step back and look squarely at the situation, it's hard not to see the absolute ridiculousness of it all. So, when they distort the narrative—like, for example, painting you as a terrible monster for doing something as healthy as setting boundaries—just imagine a silly voice in your mind saying something like, "Yes, I'm such a monster for having boundaries! My boundaries rejected you! How could I ever betray my family by taking care of myself... I am truly the greatest traitor that has ever walked on this earth! Only terrible people like me have limits and boundaries!"

Asking a narcissist to take accountability is like asking them to drink poison. Accountability is going to choke them.

Catching Yourself in a Loop of Repetitive Negative and Anxiety-Causing Thoughts

Rumination is the repetitive and persistent dwelling on past events, emotions, or experiences. It can manifest as the replaying of past situations or imagining scenarios in your mind, over and over again. It's important to become aware of rumination when it occurs as it can prevent you from dealing with your emotions directly and can be detrimental to your mental health and well-being.

When we ruminate, we tend to focus on the events that have caused us negative emotions such as anxiety, sadness, anger, and guilt. We may believe that by ruminating, we are somehow solving a problem or gaining control over a difficult situation, but in reality, rumination only keeps these emotions alive, making it harder to process and resolve them.

Additionally, rumination can prevent us from fully living in the present and immersing ourselves in the joyful moments of our daily lives. It may cause us to miss out on important experiences that hold greater value than dwelling on past toxic interactions with the narcissist and their enablers. Furthermore, it can negatively affect our relationships and hinder our ability to achieve success in our daily endeavors.

It's essential to develop the habit of catching yourself and recognizing when you are ruminating so that you can actively work towards redirecting your thoughts to healthier ways of coping.

Keep in mind that rumination is not reality and only serves to keep your mind trapped in the cycles of your past. Rumination only leads to suffering. It is like a trap with no way out.

Sometimes there really is no solution, and we must let the cards fall where they may. As soon as you become aware that you are ruminating, stop the process.

You always have the power to control the direction of your focus.

Imagine a Place That You Know

Imagining a familiar place that you know can help shift your focus away from the negative thoughts that are causing you to ruminate. Engaging in this exercise can redirect your thoughts to a logical and tangible place in your mind, rather than continuing to imagine endless scenarios with no resolution.

For example, if you find yourself ruminating about a past argument with an enabler, imagining a familiar place like the grocery store can help distract you from those negative thoughts. As you visualize the details of the store, you are essentially engaging your mind in a different activity, which can interrupt the cycle of rumination. Walk yourself through the entire store. Where are your usual items located? Visualize all the items that you put in the cart one by one.

It's essential to fully engage in the visualization exercise and use all your senses to imagine the place as vividly as possible. Pay attention to the sights, sounds, smells, and textures of the environment you are imagining. This can make the visualization more immersive and effective in shifting your focus away from rumination.

Practice Mindfulness With Your Surroundings

Practicing mindfulness with your surroundings involves using your senses to fully engage with the present moment and become more aware of your surroundings. By doing so, you can shift your focus away from ruminating thoughts and become more grounded in the present.

Look around and describe everything you see in detail. Take note of the colors, textures, shapes, and sizes of the objects in your environment. You can do this out loud or quietly in your mind, whichever feels more comfortable for you.

Another way to practice mindfulness is to engage in active listening. When talking to someone, really listen to what they are saying and try to fully understand their perspective. This can help you become more present in the conversation and shift your focus away from your own thoughts and worries.

The key to practicing mindfulness with your surroundings is to stay focused on the present moment and fully engage with your senses. This can help you become more aware of the beauty and richness of the world around you, and can also help reduce stress and anxiety by calming the mind. This practice can be done anywhere, at any time, making it a convenient tool for managing difficult emotions and thoughts.

Schedule Your Worrying Times

Scheduling your worrying times can be an effective way to manage your anxiety and prevent it from taking over your entire day. Instead of constantly worrying throughout the day, you can set aside a specific time for worrying and then focus on other tasks for the rest of the day.

To schedule your worrying times, choose a time that works best for you, such as in the morning or evening. Set aside a specific amount of time, such as 30 minutes to an hour, for worrying. During this time, allow yourself to fully focus on your worries and write them down if it helps.

Once the scheduled worrying time is over, shift your focus to other tasks and try to let go of your worries until the next scheduled time.

Journaling

Journaling is a powerful tool that can help you process and understand your thoughts, emotions, and experiences. Writing down what you've gone through and how you feel about it can help you identify patterns, work through complex emotions, and gain a new perspective on your life. Most importantly, it serves as an anchor for what happened to you. The process of putting pen to paper and reflecting on your experiences can provide a sense of catharsis and release, allowing you to feel lighter and more at peace.

Additionally, journaling is a way of acknowledging and validating your experiences, even if no one else does. Writing about what you're going through can help you recognize your own strength and resilience, serving as a reminder of how far you've come. When you look back on your journal entries in the future, you'll have a record of your growth and a source of inspiration as you continue to navigate life's ups and downs.

Journal Prompts

- When you feel gaslighted, how does it manifest in your body? Do you experience tightness in your chest, headaches, or nausea? How do these physical sensations contribute to your emotional response?
- Describe a specific interaction with someone who made you question your perception of reality. What were their specific words or actions that manipulated your sense of truth? Did this interaction cause you to doubt a specific memory or belief about yourself?
- Reflect on a situation where self-doubt held you back. Did someone's behavior contribute to your insecurities?
- Recall a time when you defied self-doubt and achieved something significant. What specific internal strengths did you utilize (e.g., resilience, perseverance)? Consider any external support that bolstered your confidence (e.g., encouragement from a friend). How can you draw on this experience and the identified strengths to build lasting self-confidence?
- What are some healthy distractions or coping mechanisms that help you stop ruminating? Write down any activities or habits that help you feel calmer and more grounded, such as exercise, meditation, or spending time in nature.

The Lessons Learned

When a person gaslights, they try to manipulate and control the other person by making them question their own reality, memories, and perceptions. They may deny things that have happened, twist facts, or blame the other person for things that are not their fault. The goal of gaslighting is to make the other person feel confused and isolated.

Using logic and proof to validate one's experiences will not be effective because the focus is not on the reality of the argument, but rather on the individual's desire to be right. Attempting to argue with someone who consistently disregards facts and evidence in order to maintain their beliefs is futile.

You must view the situation for what it really is, and accept that this person may no longer be safe for you.

Trust yourself and your own experiences. Trust your body's messages. Reach out for support from people who can validate your experiences and help you regain a sense of trust in yourself. You deserve to have your experiences and feelings validated, and you deserve to be treated with respect and kindness. Keep a journal to document any instances of gaslighting and the way it makes you feel. Continue to educate yourself about gaslighting and its effects so you can better recognize it and understand why it is happening.

If you feel crazy or confused, then take it as a sign that you are being gaslighted. There is no need to argue anymore.

Chapter 5

Boundaries

In my personal experience, I can attest that learning to set healthy boundaries for oneself for the first time can feel terrifying, even panic-inducing, as if we are doing something bad or wrong in a deeply felt sense.

As I embarked on my journey toward healing and personal growth beyond my narcissistic family system, the concept of establishing healthy boundaries was intertwined with the idea that a boundary was akin to rejecting, unintentionally hurting, or pushing away the other person. It took some time to finally understand how deeply distorted this view was. I didn't understand that a boundary was simply a line that defined my individuality from the rest of the world and that the process of laying down boundaries wasn't that big of a deal when I found yourself in healthy relationships with safe people.

Throughout my life, I had never learned how to set clear boundaries with anyone—whether it was friends, colleagues, family members, or acquaintances. How could I have? How could any of us have? Doing such a thing is considered a transgression, an insult that would inevitably lead to punishments, endless drama, guilt trips, silent treatments, and eventually full condemnation and abandonment when one comes from a narcissistic family system.

So, there is trauma associated with setting boundaries, as we are taught that boundaries lead to abandonment and betrayal. This, in turn, creates a distorted lens through which we perceive life beyond the family.

My own instinctual response was either to explode and push people away before giving them a chance to correct themselves, or to say nothing at all and allow my discomfort to fester and grow... until I was depleted. Not healthy.

The lens of guilt, shame, and false responsibility always complicates matters, making it challenging to treat oneself with respect.

In a narcissistic family system, the scapegoat's boundaries are viewed as inconveniences that can be manipulated and leveraged against them through what I call "selective giving". Family members may use a trail of breadcrumbs: occasional favors, gifts, and financial assistance for necessities to pressure the scapegoat into sacrificing their own emotional safety and individuality without considering their limits or mental health.

This pattern is reinforced by an unspoken rule:

Your individuality becomes transactional, with your silence being the currency expected in return for the occasional breadcrumbs of love, selectively given favors, or material goods, ultimately leaving no room for personal agency.

In essence, it's like saying, "Here, take what I choose to give you, and now you owe me so keep your mouth shut."

My inability to establish healthy boundaries has had a pervasive negative impact on every aspect of my life. For instance, when I first embarked on a self-employed career, my lack of self-worth and difficulty in setting boundaries caused me to make several concessions that ultimately harmed me in the long run. I wasted valuable time and resources on individuals who undervalued my worth. Similarly, in my social circle, many of the people I surrounded myself with only showed interest in me when they needed my resources, skills, or favors. However, when I reached out, I was met with vague promises of getting back to me when it suited them, or people failing to follow through on their commitments and not showing up when it mattered. I often found myself in triggering situations that left me feeling depleted and drained, yet I always responded with a resounding "yes" to everything and everyone, without considering the impact on my own well-being.

The lack of boundaries left me feeling drained of resources and energy, taken advantage of, and unable to distinguish true friends from those who were only there for the resources I could provide. It was as if I was standing alone in a crowded room, surrounded by people who claimed to care but were only interested in their own self-serving agendas.

When encircled by such an unhealthy environment, it can be bewildering and downright frightening to learn to trust oneself.

Recognize that setting boundaries may temporarily disrupt your world if your world isn't healthy for you. Those who become angry with you for setting boundaries are the ones who benefit from your lack of them. And when you lack boundaries, those are the types of people that you attract and inadvertently surround yourself with. It's a vicious circle that can feel terrifying to push through.

When I began the process of setting healthy boundaries to protect myself, my worst fears came to fruition. But through this terrifying experience, I have come to learn that when our worst fears come to pass, sometimes it isn't a bad thing, as a path is suddenly cleared and laid out before you. Setting boundaries is like turning on a light switch; suddenly, the truth is illuminated and the cockroaches scatter.

When I finally put my foot down and refused to continue tolerating toxic and abusive interactions with my mother, my enabling blood family members disowned me, while dismissing and treating my deteriorating mental health as an insignificant reason to go no contact. When I stopped providing free services and favors to acquaintances who only showed up when they wanted to access my resources, they vanished like a puff of smoke.

Prioritizing my mental health and guarding my resources and limits resulted in astonishing pushback from those around me. As I became more in tune with my non-negotiables, more and more people disappeared from my life. And finally, despite the initial shock and grief, I began to breathe fresher air.

Throughout the process, the more assertive I became with my non-negotiables, the more chaotic my world felt. People pushed back, friends disappeared, and family members treated me as a traitor. During such dark times, it's challenging not to question oneself and wonder if there's something inherently wrong with you as a person, on top of dealing with the trauma and gaslighting from the narcissistic family system.

Where is the line between reasonable and unreasonable? How do I know if I'm doing the right thing when the world around me is crumbling, when people I love dismiss me, and friends disappear? These questions led me to inquire within: How can I rely on myself to make the right decisions for myself? How can I learn to trust myself when everyone around me pushes back, gets angry, and makes me feel like my boundaries are terrible, evil things that push people away?

How can I learn to trust myself when I have been conditioned to believe that my reasoning was defective?

The solution lived within me, just as it lives within you. You will find the answer through your own thought leadership. The narrative can't solely focus on what is accepted extrinsically; instead, it must prioritize what feels right intrinsically. To distinguish right from wrong, reasonable from unreasonable, and normal from abnormal, you must get to know yourself. By focusing on your inner world, you can become conscious of your unique values, strengths, weaknesses, limits, and boundaries.

Your choices should empower you, not weaken you.

As you start asking yourself some important questions, you will begin to develop personal rules. These rules are yours alone, and it's perfectly okay if they differ from someone else's. Each person is entitled to protect themselves in their own way. You and I may not share the same values, and that's okay. This is what individuality is all about. I won't tell you what your personal rules should be because nobody has the right to decide for you. For me, creating my own set of rules became my guiding compass for a better life.

Examples of personal rules:

- Love is consistent. It doesn't turn on and off like a light switch.
- Show up when it matters that you do.
- Don't change your behavior towards me when someone else shows up.
- When you love a person, you let them know through your actions, not through your words.
- I can change my mind if I suddenly start to feel uncomfortable with a decision, as can you.
- My love is not for sale.
- I don't owe you a relationship, you don't owe me a relationship.
- My mistakes are not your weapons.
- A healthy relationship with a person isn't dependent on a relationship with a third party.
- My boundaries have nothing to do with how much I love you. Those are separate concepts.
- I am not responsible for your happiness, and you are not responsible for mine.
- Love and guilt don't work together as a team.
- Generosity and empathy are not the same thing.
- Confusion about my place in a relationship is a sign of gaslighting.
- I am not your free resource.
- Safeguarding my mental health and emotional safety takes precedence over all my decisions.

Whenever faced with self-doubt or overwhelmed by difficult emotions, rather than second guessing myself, I relied on the rules I had set for myself. These became my anchor, helping me regain center and continue forward with resolve.

When you align your actions with your values, your beliefs, your needs, your rules for better living, you will never be wrong.

Ultimately, it's not your responsibility to manage other people's reactions to your boundaries. When you set boundaries, it's likely that those who have grown accustomed to crossing them will resist the change. However, boundaries serve to protect your individuality and have nothing to do with your love for others, they have everything to do with loving yourself. Those who genuinely care about you will honor your boundaries, while those with ulterior motives will resist.

Through it all, once the mountain of doubts was crossed over, once the bad actors where sorted, I learned that setting healthy boundaries was essential for my survival and growth. It took everything I had within to take that first step, and it was heartbreaking, uncomfortable and terrifying the entire time, but beyond the temporary discomfort, is where you finally get to safety, growth and authenticity. In the end, despite the grief of losing people whom I thought genuinely loved me, it was worth it to regain control of my own life and well-being.

Always remember that as you reveal your authentic self, the world will respond in kind.

About Boundaries

A boundary is that sacred space that you hold for yourself as an individual. It acts as an invisible line that sets you apart from the rest of the world. Boundaries are normal, healthy, and protect you from harm. They are essential for the development of strong and healthy relationships. All human beings have a need for boundaries.

There are several types of boundaries that can help protect different aspects of your well-being.

- Physical boundaries are about protecting your body and personal space. They encompass your right to say no to physical touch that makes you uncomfortable, as well as ensuring that your basic physical needs like rest, nutrition, and hydration are met. These boundaries help you feel safe and secure in your physical environment.

- Emotional boundaries involve recognizing your feelings and understanding how much emotional energy you are willing to invest in others. This means being mindful of how much you share with others and setting limits to protect yourself from people who may be emotionally draining and toxic. Emotional boundaries help you maintain healthy relationships and protect your mental health.

- Intellectual boundaries involve respecting each other's thoughts, ideas, and beliefs. It means being open to different perspectives and avoiding belittling or dismissing others' ideas. Intellectual boundaries help create an environment of mutual respect and can lead to more meaningful and productive conversations.

- Sexual boundaries involve your right to make your own decisions about sexual activity and relationships. This includes respecting others' consent and communication around sexual activity. Sexual boundaries help ensure that you feel comfortable and respected in sexual situations.

- Financial boundaries involve your right to make your own financial decisions and protect yourself from financial exploitation or manipulation. This includes setting limits around spending, lending, and sharing financial information with others. Financial boundaries help ensure that you maintain your financial independence and security.

- Communication boundaries involve your right to choose how and when you communicate with others. This includes setting limits around the frequency and nature of communication and the ability to say no to certain conversations or interactions. Communication boundaries help maintain healthy relationships by ensuring that you have space for your own needs and priorities.

- Time boundaries involve your right to allocate your time according to your priorities. This includes saying no to requests or demands on your time and setting aside time for yourself. Time boundaries help ensure that you have time for self-care and personal growth.

- Psychological boundaries protect your mental health and well-being. This includes your right to peaceful living, your right to not be exposed to triggering situations, and your right to protect yourself from psychological abuse. Psychological boundaries help maintain your sense of self-worth and protect you from toxic environments.

Non-Negotiables

The general rule of thumb in healthy relationships is that boundaries are not completely rigid and may allow some degree of flexibility. In a healthy relationship, it is reasonable to make certain compromises, such as respecting each other's personal space at home, negotiating the time spent together vs alone time and also establishing who is responsible for what in order to run a household smoothly. However, there are certain non-negotiable commitments that you should never compromise, no matter who you are dealing with or what the situation is. When you honor your non-negotiables, you demonstrate self-love, self-respect, and self-honoring.

Examples of Non-Negotiables

- Not allowing physical violence.
- Not tolerating character destruction.
- Not tolerating cheating in a relationship.
- Not allowing oneself to be isolated from friends.
- Not tolerating the silent treatment.
- Not tolerating hoovering after the discard phase.
- Not tolerating any form of gaslighting.
- Not allowing oneself to engage in activities or with people that make oneself feel unsafe or uncomfortable.
- Not allowing oneself to compromise on personal values, self-care, or beliefs.
- Not allowing oneself to engage in any activity that is illegal or unethical.
- Not allowing oneself to engage in any activity that goes against one's religious or moral beliefs.
- Not allowing oneself to be belittled or talked to with disrespect.
- Not engaging with people who treat you as an inferior human being.

It's important to remember that non-negotiables are the very foundation upon which you stand and do not require an explanation on your part. Unlike healthy boundaries, which can be communicated and are flexible and adaptable, non-negotiables do not always need to be announced, especially when dealing with a narcissistic family system or an abuser. You don't need anyone's validation to establish them; you simply do it. There is no negotiation, no back and forth, no arguing about it.

Unsafe people will not respect your non-negotiables and may even ridicule, demean, and manipulate you to feel unreasonable or that something is wrong with you for upholding your boundaries. They will continue to blame your character and deflect accountability, perpetuating the cycle of abuse, no matter what you bring to the table.

I can attest to the enormous difficulty it takes for a trauma-bonded victim to advocate for their worth by honoring their non-negotiables when they are facing an entire dysfunctional narcissistic family system and going no contact alone. It's helpful to take the time to get to know your non-negotiables, write them down, and push past the fear of upholding them.

Advocating for Oneself Healthily

Advocating for oneself healthily simply does not work in narcissistic family systems. The best way to maintain boundaries in such a setting is by going gray rock, which is going to be discussed in the next chapter. Having said that, it is important to learn how to advocate for oneself healthily when one is among safe people or in professional spaces.

Enforcing boundaries can be confusing and challenging when you were never taught how to do it properly. However, there are a few strategies you can use to communicate your boundaries effectively without causing conflict or harm to others.

Use "I" Statements

When communicating your boundaries, use "I" statements instead of "you" statements. This can help the other person understand that your boundaries are personal and not an attack on them. For example, instead of saying "you always interrupt me," say "I feel disrespected when I'm interrupted."

Be Clear and Specific

Clearly communicate what your boundaries are and why they are important to you. Being specific can help the other person understand exactly what you need and why. For example, instead of saying "I need more space," say "I need at least one hour of alone time every day to recharge."

Stay Calm and Firm

It's important to stay calm and firm when communicating your boundaries, even if the other person becomes upset or defensive. Remember that your boundaries are important for your well-being, and other people's reactivity is not a good reason to suddenly drop them and expose yourself to something that violates your limits. It's okay to prioritize them

Offer Alternatives

If you're enforcing a boundary that affects someone else, offer alternatives that can help meet both of your needs. For example, if you're enforcing a boundary around your work schedule, offer to schedule a meeting at a different time that works for both of you.

Get Used to the Discomfort of Setting Boundaries

It is not uncommon to feel uncomfortable when setting boundaries, but getting comfortable with this discomfort is an important part of the process.

One way to start getting comfortable with discomfort is to remind yourself of the benefits of setting boundaries. Boundaries are a way of protecting your own needs and values, and they can lead to healthier relationships and greater self-respect. When you feel uncomfortable setting boundaries, remind yourself that you are doing something positive and important for yourself.

Another strategy is to practice setting boundaries in low-stakes situations. For example, you could start by setting a boundary with a friend about when you are available to hang out, or by politely declining a food that you don't like. These smaller, less emotionally charged situations can help you build confidence and develop your skills for setting boundaries.

It can also be helpful to have a plan for how you will respond to pushback or resistance from others. This might involve rehearsing what you will say, or thinking through different scenarios and how you will handle them. Remember that it is normal to feel anxious or uncomfortable when facing resistance, but having a plan can help you stay focused on your goals and maintain your boundaries.

Be Assertive, Not Aggressive

Understanding the difference between assertive and aggressive behavior is essential when it comes to setting and upholding boundaries.

Assertive behavior involves communicating one's needs and boundaries in a clear, direct, and respectful way. It requires being confident and firm in expressing oneself without resorting to aggression, manipulation, or hostility. The goal is to stand up for yourself while also respecting the needs and boundaries of others.

On the other hand, aggressive behavior involves attempting to control or dominate others through force, intimidation, or coercion. Instead of approaching the situation as a discussion, it is approached as a direct attack, where one may react feeling as if they are directly threatened. One must become aware of their triggers and how they manifest physically so that one may detect if they are inadvertently setting boundaries in an aggressive manner, which can, in fact, be quite off-putting when trying to advocate for oneself in a healthy relationship.

When it comes to setting and upholding boundaries, assertive behavior is the healthy approach. Assertive communication allows you to express your needs and boundaries in a clear and direct way without resorting to aggression or hostility. This can establish mutual respect and understanding in relationships, leading to more fulfilling and satisfying connections with others.

Journal Prompts

- Think about a specific instance when you felt like your boundaries were not respected. What were the circumstances and how did you respond?
- Reflect on patterns in your relationships where your boundaries were consistently disregarded. What are the common themes or triggers in these situations?
- Consider a time when you struggled to set a boundary in a relationship. What were the reasons for this and how did it make you feel?
- What are some physical sensations or symptoms that you experience when your boundaries are crossed? How do these sensations contribute to your emotional response?
- Think about a specific relationship or interaction that consistently challenges your boundaries. What are the specific actions or behaviors of the other person that make you feel uncomfortable or disrespected?
- What are the most important things to you in life right now?
- Write about a time when you had to stood up for yourself, even if it meant going against the norm or facing resistance. What strengths did you draw on?

The Lessons Learned

In a narcissistic family system, the concept of setting boundaries is often distorted, seen as selfish or unacceptable, even though they themselves impose upon you their narratives of what lines you may not cross with them, and what lines they can cross as they please with you. It's a catch-22. However, if that's the narrative they choose to paint, then so be it. It's time to embrace a bit of selfishness.

The term "selfish" carries the connotation of solely focusing on oneself, directing attention inward, and aligning with our own needs, wants, and desires regardless of the people in our midst. It involves making choices that are in our best interest, ensuring we retain what we need without depleting ourselves for others.

Amidst the chaos and manipulation, understanding that establishing boundaries is necessary for one's well-being is paramount. It's about prioritizing mental and emotional health in the face of toxicity.

Embracing boundaries as an act of self-care involves realizing that it's okay to prioritize oneself. It's about setting limits to protect one's energy, emotions, and sanity from constant intrusion and manipulation without guilt or shame.

By reshaping the narratives and dynamics surrounding your boundaries, you're affirming your authenticity in a healthy manner. This act is a profound form of self-care, serving as a means to reclaim your inherent power and agency.

Know that you possess the strength to honor yourself, to assert limits, and to carve out space for your healing and growth as you journey forward.

Chapter 6

The Gray Rock Method

I don't think I'll be teaching you anything new by stating that traditional methods of setting boundaries don't work with narcissistic people or their enablers.

Something that isn't always discussed is that there are circumstances under which speaking up, even if done according to the rules, simply doesn't change the outcome of a toxic relationship.

Even carefully constructed "I" statements, waiting for the right time, focusing on actions rather than attacking the person, and so on, will not produce the desired outcome.

This is because sometimes the problem isn't rooted in how you deliver the information but in the other person's ability or lack thereof to listen.

Therefore, if you find yourself in a situation where you must still interact with the narcissist or their flying monkeys, the most appropriate approach is to utilize the gray rock method.

What to Expect from a Narcissist When You Lay Down Boundaries

- They will violate your boundaries to get a rise out of you.
- They will gaslight you.
- They will play victim and claim that your boundaries are hurting them.
- They will ridicule you.
- They will call you controlling.
- They will call you manipulative.
- They will make you feel unreasonable.
- They will make you feel guilty.
- They will shame you.

The gray rock method may feel as formidable challenge that requires immense self-discipline and emotional control for survivors of narcissistic abuse.

Narcissists are adept at twisting reality, often using the reactions of their victims to discredit their character and create the illusion that there is something wrong with them. They will do and say anything to avoid taking accountability for the conflicts that they initiate in the first place.

However, always remember that your reactions give the narcissist their ammunition. Their fights are not logical, they are inventions designed to for one purpose: To quench their need for supply.

You need to detach yourself from every personal insult, lie, gaslighting attempt, and especially from having your vulnerabilities weaponized and used against you. You must become the observer of a very intriguing horror show, but refrain from stepping onto the stage. Avoid reacting. Simply observe and detach.

They may continue to challenge your cool for some time, but eventually, as you continue on with this technique, they may eventually get bored with you and look for an easier source of supply elsewhere.

Think of it this way: Have you ever witnessed a

street race? The way the cars rev up their engines, and as the countdown starts, they become louder and louder, awaiting the opportunity to unleash their speed and power. With a narcissist, antagonism functions in precisely the same manner.

It may take time to master this technique, however, with consistent practice, the gray rock method can be an incredibly effective tool. By learning to stay calm and neutral, you can avoid falling into their trap and protect yourself from the escalation of their abusive tactics. By staying calm, you do not enter the stage that they are setting for you.

At the end of the day, it's important to recognize that their behavior is a reflection of their own issues and has nothing to do with your worth or value as a person.

This is the world they choose to inhabit, but it doesn't have to be your reality. By refusing to engage in their manipulative games, you can shield yourself from providing them with ammunition to use against you. Don't let the narcissist's illusions distort your self-perception. There's no need to engage in arguments. Keep in mind that your silence, when employed as a shield to safeguard yourself, is a powerful way to establish healthy boundaries. It's important not to confuse your silence, utilized for self-protection against further psychological harm, with the narcissist's silent treatments, which are intended to cause pain.

How to Gray Rock

Observe, detach, disengage.

By disengaging emotionally and mentally, you create a shield against their attempts to provoke a reaction.

Disengaging Means:

- Withholding Personal Information: Refrain from sharing details about your inner world, including your thoughts, feelings, projects, passions, relationships, problems, and victories. This limits the toxic person's access to information they could potentially use against you.

- Guarding Emotions: Avoid displaying emotional reactions, as toxic individuals often feed off such responses. By maintaining emotional composure, you reduce the likelihood of providing them with the satisfaction they seek.

- Limiting Interaction: Minimize direct communication and interaction whenever possible. This could involve reducing the frequency of meetings, phone calls, or any form of engagement that allows the toxic person to influence or manipulate you.

- Redirecting Conversations: Steer conversations away from sensitive topics or those that may trigger negative reactions. Redirect discussions toward neutral subjects that minimize the potential for conflict or manipulation.

- Maintaining Consistency: Stay consistent in your disengagement efforts. Toxic individuals may test boundaries or attempt to draw you back into their drama, so it's essential to remain steadfast in your commitment to distance yourself.

Gray rocking often involves behaviors like:
- Shrugging and nodding.
- Remain calm and serene.
- Not engaging.
- Using short phrases and non-committal responses like "uh-huh".

- Avoiding eye contact.
- Responding briefly, without defending yourself or explaining anything.
- Ending or leaving interactions as quickly as is safely possible.

The Yellow Rock Method

Kill them with kindness?

The yellow rock method is a spin on the gray rock method. It involves using positivity as a tool by adding some niceties to gray rock communication. Its name comes from the idea that a yellow rock appears friendlier, warmer and more inviting than a gray rock. However, it is still ultimately gray rock and unlikely to hold a narcissist's interest for a prolonged period.

Yellow rocking often involves behaviors like:

- Smiling and nodding, giving off an "innocently positive vibe".
- Play dumb. Make them think they are smarter than you.
- Using short phrases with a positive spin like "I'll do my best!", 'Everything is great, no worries!" "It's so lovely to hear from you!" "Thank you for sharing your thoughts with me, I appreciate your honesty" or "I would love to help you if I could!"
- Responding briefly, without defending yourself or explaining anything.
- Ending or leaving interactions as quickly as is safely possible.

Reject the Energy That You Do Not Want in Your Orbit

While the Gray Rock Method is an effective safeguarding tool, it can be emotionally draining to apply as you try to appear uninterested while a toxic person invades your space and tries to extract supply from you. By adding a spiritual dimension to your practice, you can make this method more effective and reduce its impact on your mental health.

Visualization Technique

1. Draw your focus inward and mentally summon back all of your scattered energy that rightfully belongs to you. Center it in a potent power point within your being.
2. Take a deep breath, and with your mind's eye, acknowledge the negative energy that is attempting to infiltrate your space. Visualize it as a separate sphere, black and murky, far removed from your own vibrant energy bubble. Allow the clear divide between the two energies to settle, forming a protective barrier that shields you from the toxic influence.
3. Listen to your body, and pay attention to the subtle signals that alert you to the presence of the toxic energy. Acknowledge its presence, and with a gentle yet firm intention, release it back to its source. As you do, envision it flowing away from you like a stream, taking with it any remnants of negativity that may have lingered. Focus inward, and allow yourself to bask in the peace and clarity of your own energy field.
4. Finally, as you stand in the midst of your own protective shield, visualize an energy bubble that separates your energy from the source of toxicity. Allow it to expand outward, surrounding you in a glowing orb of safety and protection. With each breath, draw strength and clarity from the power within.

No Magic Cure to Change Narcissism

While the gray rock Method serves as a tool to protect your well-being, it's important to recognize that it is not a magical solution.

The gray rock method is unlikely to alter a person's mentality, beliefs, or cure emotional dysregulation. It remains a self-preservation strategy rather than a transformative remedy for the underlying issues in a toxic person.

Things to Be Aware Of When Implementing the Gray Rock Method:

Escalation of Behavior

In certain situations, when a toxic person perceives that their usual tactics are not eliciting the expected emotional response, they may escalate their efforts to regain control. This escalation can take various forms, such as heightened manipulation, guilt-tripping, personal attacks, character destruction, leveraging past mistakes to control the present situation, aggression, or deliberate attempts to provoke a reaction. It's important to acknowledge that, under such circumstances, seeking help, contacting authorities, and implementing complete no-contact measures may be the most prudent course of action, especially if the situation poses a danger or significantly impacts one's mental health.

Temporary 'Fake' Improvement

Initially, the gray rock method may lead to a reduction in negative interactions, but it might not necessarily lead to long-term behavioral change in the narcissist. They may temporarily modify their behavior to regain your attention or trust and when they feel like you are fully invested in the relationship once again, they will revert back to their old ways.

Isolation and Loneliness

Implementing the gray rock method requires minimizing interactions and creating emotional distance not only with the toxic individual but also with those who enable their behavior. This includes all "well-meaning" messengers and enablers who downplay your experiences to maintain the established hierarchy or the status quo. While the gray rock is a powerful tool for self-protection, these measures can lead to feelings of isolation and loneliness. Therefore, it becomes even more important to establish a support system during this period to counterbalance these emotions and navigate the challenges of distancing yourself from toxic dynamics.

Potential Backlash

Some individuals may react negatively to the perceived lack of engagement, interpreting it as rejection or abandonment. This could lead to backlash in the form of gossip, spreading rumors, or attempts to damage your reputation. For instance, disengaging might lead the narcissistic parent to accuse you of being ungrateful, distant, or lacking family orientation. Unable to elicit a direct reaction from you, they may resort to distorting reality and playing the victim, influencing other family members to reach out to you, deliver speeches, and attempt to draw you back in. The narcissistic parent might even claim to be 'broken-hearted,' employing deeply disturbing manipulation tactics designed to divide the family and conquer.

Not Suitable for All Situations:

The gray rock method may not be suitable for all situations or relationships. In cases of severe abuse or danger, seeking professional help or involving authorities may be necessary.

In the Aftermath

While detachment is an ideal solution in theory, emotionally, it is easier said than done.

It's vital to carve out a sacred space for yourself, establishing a protective bubble where only safe individuals are allowed. These safe individuals are often those with no connection to the narcissistic person. Equally important is actively engaging in activities that bring you joy, pursuing passion projects, and focusing on personal development despite lingering feelings of heaviness, grief, and injustice.

Allow yourself to process and express your emotions in a safe and private space. This may involve engaging in healthy coping mechanisms such as crying it out, confiding in a trusted friend, journaling, painting, running, weightlifting, or venting frustrations on a punching bag with loud music playing in the background—whatever helps you release pent-up emotions and regain a sense of peace.

I must caution you, as much as these interactions hurt, avoid engaging in self-destructive behavior in the aftermath. Do not let them continue to have power over you or your life by engaging in any self-destructive outlets and hurting yourself. Every time that you engage in self-destructive and self-sabotaging behavior, they win.

Instead, use their negative behavior to motivate yourself to become a better and healthier version of yourself. Use their negativity as fuel to push yourself to achieve your goals, and to distance yourself from their toxic influence.

When they try to minimize or attack you, hold onto your identity and inner strength. Remember that their words and actions are a reflection of their own insecurities and flaws, and have nothing to do with your worth or capabilities. Instead of letting their negativity bring you down, let it inspire you to rise above their behavior and become your best self.

As you continue to build a happy and fulfilling life for yourself, it's important to keep the narcissist and their enablers out of your inner world. Acknowledge your emotions and process them, but don't allow them to consume you or give the narcissist power over your thoughts and feelings. Recognize the unhealthy pattern of the relationship and choose to focus your energy and attention on creating a positive and healthy environment for yourself. This is how true justice will be served. And while you refuse to play their game, and focus on living a harmonious and peaceful life, a narcissist will continue to be a narcissist, and their destructive ways will carry on without you.

Journal Prompts

- Describe recent interactions that felt toxic. How did you feel during these interactions? What triggers or patterns did you notice?
- Explore your emotional responses to toxic interactions. Are there specific emotions that arise frequently? How do these emotions manifest in your body?
- Define what practicing the gray rock method means to you. What behaviors will you adopt to minimize engagement and emotional reactions during interactions?
- List self-care activities that help you feel grounded and centered. How can you incorporate these practices into your daily routine to support yourself?
- Are there boundaries you need to reinforce? List them all.

The Lessons Learned

When engaging in discussions with others, our aim is often to resolve conflicts, dispel misunderstandings, and establish healthy boundaries, which are crucial for the growth of any healthy relationship. However, resorting to the gray rock method indicates that we have lost hope for authentic communication, being listened to, and gave up on any meaningful relationship growth with the other person.

We resort to the gray rock method because the person in question has persistently demonstrated a lack of regard for our feelings, emotions, boundaries, and opinions, and holds a rigid and biased view of themselves and the world as the only truth.

Narcissists will paint your boundaries as an attack. Unfortunately, even if a narcissistic parent's actions have led to their child developing serious troubles such as anxiety or panic disorders in adulthood, they are unlikely to acknowledge or reflect on their behavior. Even when presented with evidence of harm they've caused, narcissistic parents will dismiss their child's distress as mere performance, depriving them of the love and concern they deserve.

The narcissist will prioritize their god-like image of perfection over having a genuine and healthy relationship with another person, even if it's their own child.

In a relationship with a narcissist, there is never a level playing field, and sharing your emotions, limits, boundaries and hurt is metamorphosed into a rivalry of "who is more pained." or "explaining their motives for disregarding your boundaries." or "informing you of their knowledge being superior to yours." Striving to reason with a narcissist is a vain effort. It is impossible to compel someone to change their hurtful ways towards you or treat you with civility when they are unwilling to do so.

In a healthy relationship, both sides strive for mutual comprehension and there is a reciprocal interchange that allows for self-improvement and relationship growth. In a detrimental one sided relationship with a narcissist, often the only solution is to emotionally disengage and find more nourishing relationships elsewhere.

I firmly stand by the statement that emotional detachment from a narcissistic parent is your best form of protection.

Remember, it's not normal for someone to constantly create conflict and make you feel small. You deserve to be surrounded by people who uplift and support you, and to live a life that brings you joy and fulfillment. Don't let the narcissist fool you into thinking that you are the role they have assigned for you. Instead, use their negativity to propel yourself forward and watch as you flourish and thrive without them. Their world is an illusion, a mere act, a performance. You don't need to set foot on that stage, play the role they want you to play, or follow the script they have written for you ever again.

Sit back and observe, much like an audience member at a circus. In this spectacle, you witness flying monkeys, lions jumping through hoops, clowns entertaining the crowd, all under the watchful eye of a shady ringmaster orchestrating the entire show.

Chapter 7

The Toxic Cycles That Keep Us Trapped

Leaving It All Behind

Throughout my life, I've made several attempts to break free from the toxic familial dynamics I found myself in, only to find myself drawn back in time and again. Initially, I berated myself for this pattern, feeling foolish, stupid, and weak for succumbing to it repeatedly. However, it eventually dawned on me that my inability to escape this cycle was not uncommon or unexpected. Scapegoats, like myself, are subjected to psychological manipulation from a young age, causing us to internalize feelings of guilt, shame, self-doubt, and worthlessness. This manipulation makes it challenging to recognize the abuse we endure deep within our senses, to believe, with our body, mind, and soul, that we deserve better treatment, and most importantly that we can trust ourselves.

The truth is that the instinctual pull for a child to return home is incredibly powerful, often overshadowing logical reasoning, especially during moments of vulnerability and despair. From my own experience, this pull occurred far too frequently, particularly during times of trouble when seeking refuge at home felt like the only viable option. It was sometimes driven by my affection and empathy for "the good parent," or the tendency of others to consistently downplay the situation, leading me to question whether I had truly been abused or not. There were occasions when I received gifts and enjoyed pleasant times with the designated golden child, who would often dismiss the severity of the situation by laughing it off or saying things like, "She's crazy with me too, just ignore her..." without recognizing the stark contrast in treatment between us. His tactics to silence me by changing the subject, laughing it off, or blatantly telling me that he didn't want to hear about it anymore, from my young teen years all the way through my adulthood would only further trigger deep feelings of shame within me.

The scapegoat's internal turmoil stems from the battle between the conditioning they are pushed to believe, that their dysfunctional environment is normal, and their own instincts which tell them that this is all wrong.

Going no contact is not merely about escaping one abuser; it's about breaking free from an entire system that shields them, trivializes our experiences, and normalizes dysfunction. We are essentially fighting against our environment, the environment that we were born into—a system that we were raised in and that acts as a bubble, preventing us from seeing what is healthy, what is not, what is real, what is not, what is abuse, and what is love, what is the truth, and what is a lie, what is authentic, and what is not.

For me, the decision to go no contact with my mother wasn't one I could make lightly as it is for any survivor who decides to go no contact. The choice for a scapegoat often boils down to persisting in trying to maintain ties, despite the toll it takes on their mental health, emotional well-being and physical safety, or taking the daunting step of leaving and confronting the reality of isolation, exclusion, and smear campaigns that will inevitably be directed at them in the aftermath. The narrative that will then be painted by the family, portraying them as heartless individuals who abandoned their loved ones, is a stark irony considering the rejection and isolation that the scapegoat faced their entire life.

When your experiences are consistently invalidated, and you find yourself repeatedly defending your trauma, pain, and truth, it creates a profound sense of shock that can feel nearly insurmountable to process and overcome. I came to realize that this feeling was rooted in betrayal, which becomes exceptionally challenging to reconcile and heal from when compounded by years of narcissistic abuse. The abuser frequently initiates endless debates and competitions, fostering a "they said vs. they said" dynamic where the victim's voice is drowned out. Engaging in such debates becomes futile for the scapegoat, who is already positioned at the bottom of the family hierarchy, especially when the abuser consistently claims victimhood themselves.

It's a harsh reality to face—that there's no family, no clan protection, and no friends or allies—especially if ties to the central family figure who scapegoated them still exist.

The Internal Experience Of Going No Contact

When scapegoats make the decision to go no contact with their narcissistic family, it's natural for them to experience a range of emotions. Firstly, there may be a profound sense of relief as they finally break free from the toxic environment that has plagued them for so long, providing a feeling of liberation and freedom.

However, this relief may be accompanied by feelings of guilt, as they grapple with the notion of cutting off contact with family members, even if it's for their own well-being. Alongside these conflicting emotions, there may be a deep sadness as they mourn the loss of what could have been a healthy and loving family relationship, despite the reality of its toxicity.

Moreover, anger may arise towards the narcissistic family members for the years of abuse and manipulation endured, fueling a desire for justice and accountability. Yet, intertwined with these emotions is fear, as they worry about potential backlash or retaliation from family members due to their decision to sever ties.

There may be moments of loneliness as they miss the idea of having a supportive family, despite knowing that the relationship was harmful. There may even be the occasional powerful urge to break no-contact out of a deep, desperate, burning need to hold on to hope, be loved, seen, heard, and validated.

My advice is for you to resist your desperate impulses; you will not find peace in the same place that keeps destroying it. Emotions can change, but pattens do not lie.

Beware of Euphoric Recall

Euphoric recall is a well-documented phenomenon that can occur in abusive relationships, particularly those involving trauma bonding. In these situations, the victim may hold onto fond memories of the abuser and the relationship, despite the abuse they have endured.

This is often fueled by the abuser's manipulative tactics. They may use intermittent reinforcement, showering the victim with affection, promises, gifts, or kind gestures after periods of abuse. These "good times" create a confusing cycle, making the abuse seem less severe and offering a glimmer of hope for change. Enablers within the system may also downplay or even deny the abuse, further blurring the lines for the victim.

For a scapegoat in a narcissistic family system, this

euphoric recall can be particularly damaging. They may grapple with intense anger and resentment towards their family, yet cling to these positive memories. This dissonance can lead to feelings of guilt and shame, making them question their decision to leave the dysfunctional dynamic. They may feel confused about their role in the family and the true nature of the relationships.

Euphoric recall can be a significant obstacle to healing from abuse. It's important to remember that these positive memories are not an accurate reflection of reality.

Toxic Cycles

Narcissists often manipulate their children through a predictable cycle of idealization, devaluation, and discard. It's no secret that this pattern can be incredibly confusing and damaging for any developing child.

It's important to note that these stages may not happen in a linear fashion, and they might overlap. The experiences will also vary widely depending on the type of narcissist. The following cycle is an example that mirrors my own upbringing, and I encourage you to become aware of and write about the toxic loops that you have experienced within your own narcissistic family system.

The Idealization Stage

The idealization stage for a scapegoat within a narcissistic family system can be a bewildering and contradictory experience. Initially, the narcissistic parent may lavish the scapegoat with affection and attention, much like they would with a "golden child." These initial positive interactions may instill a sense of security and belonging in the scapegoat.

However, this idealization comes with conditions. The level of affection bestowed upon the scapegoat is dictated by the narcissistic parent's needs, desires, and the image they wish to project to the world.

As a result, the scapegoat may receive conflicting messages right from their earliest interactions. They might be praised and "shown off" one minute, like a little trophy, only to be subtly undermined or sabotaged the next, leading to a dissonance that undermines their trust in their own perception of reality.

As the child may yearn for the love and approval of the parent, they may also simultaneously dread the unpredictable outbursts and emotional neglect that they begin to be subjected to when the parent isn't happy. The inconsistent and narcissistic parenting will eventually take a toll on the scapegoat's self-esteem.

While the idealization stage may appear positive on the surface, it ultimately ensnares the scapegoat in a trap. It fosters a false sense of hope and impedes their ability to recognize abuse as they grow older. This stage lays the groundwork for a lifelong struggle with self-doubt, codependency, and difficulty in forming healthy attachments.

My own upbringing provides a clear illustration of this dynamic. There are numerous videos and photographs captured by my father that seemingly depict moments of joy and happiness during my childhood and even adulthood. Sometimes, he would gather me to watch these "cherished memories" as a way to reassure me of my mother's love, especially following episodes where her actions triggered my panic disorder, resulting in uncontrollable physical reactions. However, rather than acknowledging these reactions as valid responses to distress, they were often dismissed as irrational tantrums. Instead, my father would emphasize the presence of "love" within our dysfunctional household by highlighting these seemingly happy moments, as if they could somehow outweigh or nullify the impact of the abuse.

But are these moments truly happy? While labeling them as "happy" may be a stretch, it's true that there may be good times amidst the dysfunction.

Narcissistic abuse is not always obvious as it can be cyclical. This coming and going of "happy" moments is precisely why it becomes so difficult for victims to truly grasp the reality of their situation.

The Devaluation Stage

The happy facade eventually crumbles as the scapegoat is singled out and enters the devaluation stage. This is when the once "special little one" begins to notice the fractures in the family dynamic. They might start expressing their opinions, challenging the unreasonable expectations imposed by the narcissistic parent, or asserting their individuality against the parent's desire for control. However, this newfound sense of self is met with a chilling response.

The affectionate gaze of the narcissistic parent turns icy. The scapegoat's emotional needs and desires are disregarded, mocked, or met with feigned indifference. Guilt and shame become potent weapons, manipulated to coerce the child back into submission.

The child's perceived "defiance" triggers a campaign of devaluation. The narcissistic parent, aided by enablers within the family, unleashes a barrage of criticism, blaming the child's personality, behavior, stubbornness, or emotions for their own emotional dysregulation and persistent unhappiness. The scapegoat becomes an easy target, blamed for everything that goes wrong. Their individuality, once tolerated, is now viewed as a threat to the narcissist's control.

As the scapegoat grows older, their teenage and young adult aspirations become battlegrounds. Their goals and dreams are met with scorn and indifference. Their unique perspective and emotional expression are seen as inconvenient truths that disrupt the carefully constructed family facade. Interests and hobbies are discouraged, supplanted by a predetermined path dictated by the narcissist.

Meanwhile, the golden child may enjoy favoritism and encouragement, exacerbating the contrast and leaving the scapegoat feeling inadequate and incapable. The constant negativity fosters a sense of being trapped, unfulfilled, and directionless.

The Discard Stage

During their teenage and young adult years, the narcissistic parent may escalate their abuses on the scapegoat. The consistent attacks and relentless antagonisms prompt the scapegoat to become highly reactive. Attempts to minimize contact with the narcissistic parent, and even attempts to flee are perceived as rebellious acts that occur for "mysterious reasons" by the rest of the family.

In response to the scapegoat's resistance, the narcissistic parent may resort to punitive measures, frequently discarding them. This could involve giving the silent treatment, where the parent completely ignores their child for prolonged periods of time, while simultaneously claiming worry and victimhood to anyone who listens.

This ongoing dynamic can be profoundly traumatic, resulting in lasting damage to the scapegoat's self-esteem and mental well-being.

Moreover, the discard stage can engender a profound sense of displacement in the scapegoat's life. They may struggle to establish healthy relationships and find it challenging to connect with their own identity. The constant cycle of rejection and abandonment can erode their trust in others and hinder their ability to form meaningful connections. Alternatively, it may drive them to seek validation from anyone who shows them attention, rendering them vulnerable to exploitation by manipulators outside the narcissistic family structure.

The Hoovering Stage

If the scapegoat leaves, or minimizes contact, the narcissistic family may use various tactics to try and lure the scapegoat back into the family dynamic. These tactics are harmful and manipulative.

Here are some examples of the tactics that may be used during the hoovering stage:

Love-Bombing

After a period of coldness or rejection, the scapegoat may be lured back in by a calculated campaign known as love-bombing. This deceptive tactic involves a sudden shower of affection, compliments, and gifts. The message is clear: "Come back, we love you!" However, beneath this facade lies a manipulative agenda designed to:

- Reignite Yearning: The sudden shift in behavior taps into the scapegoat's natural desire for connection and love. After experiencing isolation and neglect, the scapegoat may be vulnerable to believing this newfound affection is genuine.

- Erode Boundaries: The love-bombing softens the scapegoat's defenses, making them more susceptible to manipulation. Boundaries that were previously established may begin to crumble, leaving the scapegoat open to future abuse.

- Distort Reality: The intense affection creates a confusing dissonance with past experiences. The scapegoat may begin to doubt their own memories and perceptions, questioning if the abuse was ever that bad.

- Regain Control: Ultimately, the goal of love-bombing is to regain control of the scapegoat. Once the scapegoat is back in the fold, the cycle of abuse can begin anew.

Love-bombing is particularly insidious because it preys on the scapegoat's emotional vulnerabilities. The desire for connection and the hope that things can change can be powerful motivators. However, remember that this affection is not genuine. It's a temporary performance.

Flying Monkeys

The narcissistic family member may enlist the involvement of a third party, be it another family member or friend, in their efforts to pass on messages of "concern" or communicate their "feelings" with the scapegoat. By doing so, they aim to induce feelings of guilt within the scapegoat for not acquiescing to their demands or for "causing discord" with the third party by not complying.

Despite their seemingly "neutral" stance, flying monkeys serve to perpetuate the narcissist's agenda and are not safe allies for the scapegoat.

They might say things like, "Don't you love your family?" or "Why are you tearing the family apart?" They may try to rationalize the narcissist's actions, claiming that they mean well and miss the scapegoat terribly. Such statements are designed to manipulate the scapegoat into feeling guilty for setting boundaries or seeking distance from the toxic family environment.

Sudden Requests for Help

After a period of silence or ostracization, the scapegoat may be surprised by a sudden request for help from a family member. This seemingly olive branch often masks a web of manipulation. These requests are rarely genuine attempts at reconciliation, but rather calculated maneuvers designed to:

- Reassert Control: By asking for help, the family member subtly attempts to regain power over the scapegoat. They remind the scapegoat of their "obligation" to the family unit, chipping away at boundaries that have been set.

- Disregard Past Abuse: The casual nature of the request ignores the emotional trauma inflicted on the scapegoat. It's as if the abuse never happened.

- Guilt Trip and Exploit: The family member may resort to guilt-tripping, reminding the scapegoat of past favors or sacrifices made on their behalf.

- Create Confusion: The sudden shift from silence to requesting help can be incredibly confusing and frustrating for the scapegoat. It creates a sense of cognitive dissonance, leaving them questioning if they should comply.

- Trap the Scapegoat: If the scapegoat refuses the request, they are then painted as the villain – the one who is "rejecting" their loving family. This manipulation tactic deflects blame and keeps the scapegoat trapped in the cycle of abuse.

The core issue stems from the narcissist's distorted sense of entitlement. They harbor the belief that the world owes them something, yet they consistently disregard the needs, feelings, and experiences of the scapegoated child. This unbalanced dynamic ensures that any assistance offered by the narcissist comes with strings attached, while any support or aid they receive is viewed as rightfully theirs, simply because they believe they are entitled to it. This entitlement-driven mentality perpetuates a toxic cycle wherein the scapegoat is continually manipulated and exploited for the narcissist's benefit, without any genuine consideration for their well-being.

Toxic Gifts and Holiday Cards

Gifts may be sent by mail or dropped off at the door on special occasions such as birthdays or holidays. The purpose of these gifts is never genuine love; rather, they are just another manipulation tactic meant to confuse the scapegoat into feeling guilty for setting healthy boundaries for themselves. These gifts are, in fact, weapons. Their message is: "See? We still love you despite your horrible character, despite how unlovable you are, and despite the fact that you rejected us after everything that we did for you. Look at how good we are. We are still here, waiting for your return because we are selfless, caring, and good while you are evil, ungrateful, and irrational."

The Return

If the scapegoat decides to return to the family fold, it is highly likely that the same dynamics that have always unfolded will carry on as if the scapegoat never left.

Journal Prompt

- Reflect on the toxic cycle within your narcissistic family system, considering the example provided.

- Recall a specific relationship or interaction where you felt trapped in an unhealthy pattern. Describe in detail the actions or behaviors of the other person that contributed to your sense of entrapment. Contrast what made you stay in the situation versus what made you want to leave.

- Evaluate the influence of enablers in your life on the toxic cycle within your family. Identify those who have enabled the narcissist in your life. Describe their contributions to keeping you within reach of your abuser, and examine the nature of the attachment you hold for them.

The Lessons Learned

Take some time to decipher the toxic patterns of your narcissistic family system; know that history repeats itself and patterns never lie.

Remember, there is a difference between giving the silent treatment as a means to punish, and distancing yourself from an unsafe person to protect yourself. The silent treatment is cruel, comes from a place of immaturity, and is designed to punish and inflict pain. It is emotional abuse. On the other hand, going no contact is setting a healthy boundary to protect yourself from further harm; it comes from a place of wisdom, and it is an act of self-preservation.

Recognizing and understanding the toxic patterns in your narcissistic family system is crucial for your healing and personal growth. Being aware of these patterns can help you to identify and avoid harmful behavior, and to make informed decisions about your relationships.

Furthermore, become mindful of any euphoric recall that you may experience as you withdraw, especially if you find yourself alone and feeling lonely. Recognize that these feelings are normal. The bond formed in abusive relationships is often a result of the good moments that exist alongside the bad. This is what makes leaving the cycle of abuse so difficult. By acknowledging and validating these feelings, you can be kinder and more understanding towards yourself.

Healing from abuse and breaking the trauma bond takes time. Remember that there may be moments of fond memories during this process, and it's ok to have them. These positive memories should be acknowledged, but it is important to understand that they do not negate the abuse. Safe relationships are built on mutual trust, respect, and safety, and do not use "the good times" and "favors" as leverage to control the other person.

Chapter 8

Understanding Your Emotions

The path to processing emotions healthily, connecting with oneself, and trusting one's instincts is incredibly difficult after having experienced being raised by a narcissist.

Sometimes, after provoking me and fabricating a conflict, in a bewildering turn my mother would suddenly prepare a meal, press a juice, or do my laundry, bringing it to my room while I was still reeling from the encounter. Despite giving me the silent treatment, she would, with a hurt tone, interject with comments like, "Here, even though you don't deserve this," as she handed me whatever she prepared, exited the room, and carried on with the silent treatment for indefinite periods of time. I could hear her sigh as if martyred and forced into such acts of care.

I soon began to feel disgust around my mother, and this sensation of disgust was then accompanied by feelings of guilt, shame, and confusion.

Growing up, I couldn't make sense out of what she was doing and why. However, what I did know was that if I declined her offerings or stated that I wasn't hungry or thirsty, it would lead to a whole new level of drama and screaming. Other family members would then be told by her that she nicely made me a juice and I ungratefully rejected it. On the other hand, accepting her gestures meant they would later be weaponized against me, especially when other family members were present, reminding me of her supposed kindness when she sought to assert control. "I gave you a nice hot meal yesterday. After everything I do for you, this is how you treat your poor mother?"

She successfully trained me to have no safe space for my own emotions in my own body. I felt trapped, experiencing heightened urges to fight, flee, or numb myself and dissociate. Emotionally, there was nowhere to turn.

I came to grasp that she felt entitled to inflict hurt because of how she herself was feeling on any given day. Her triggers gave her a pass to do whatever she wanted. She was entitled to hurt because she was "a victim". And so I had to become a very good student of her moods, and began being able to detect what was coming at me just from her body posture, the way that she walked, the way that she looked at me, even from the way that she sat and watched tv.

It was her victimhood narrative that defined her entire existence, that excused the things she did, and that was then used to create impossible expectations that I simply did not have the power to fulfill or fight against.

I deduced from her actions towards me that she believed I possessed no feelings worthy of acknowledgment. In her eyes, my feelings were merely a direct competition against hers, where the winner was the one "who suffered most." Any expression of pain on my part was promptly dismissed as attention-seeking behavior unworthy of recognition. How dare I express anything other than joy in her angelic presence? How ungrateful of a child I was.

Moreover, any sense of frustration or exasperation on my part was construed as a personal attack, even if those emotions originated from unrelated events, such as having a challenging day at school, or as I previously mentioned, breaking my leg.

The only acceptable expression permitted in her presence was a constant smile; even if she never wore one, and even after a beating.

When one is raised to believe that their normal human emotions are "evil" and the reason for the abuses they endure, an inevitable fragmentation occurs within. There's a sense of believing that your natural instincts, instincts inherent in every human since the beginning of humanity, are flawed, and thus, we disconnect from ourselves.

For many survivors, understanding why we feel what we feel, or even identifying our emotions in the first place, can be challenging. Therefore, comprehending our emotional world is a huge aspect of the healing process.

Allowing myself to name my emotions and to finally embrace them was like rediscovering a lost part of myself. I learned to create a safe haven within me, a place where I could truly feel again, without fear or judgment.

By learning how emotions are processed, understanding triggers, and recognizing how feelings operate, we can regain control over our reactions and restore a sense of balance in our lives.

A Lesson on Emotions

Emotions are part of our instincts. They are natural and a normal part of being human. They provide valuable and immediate information about what is good, what is bad and what is dangerous. They are designed to alert us to dangers or rewards and are a primitive instinct that exists within us for the purpose of our survival. Emotions manifest physically, and can be detected or measured. For example, when you experience an emotion, you may get a high heartbeat, you may sweat, your blood pressure will rise, and you may shake.

Now, the problem with emotions is that because they are instinctual, they do not always have all the information necessary to make rational and healthy long term decisions.

Imagine you have a big project due tomorrow and have informed everyone not to disturb you. You've turned off your phone, placed a "Do Not Disturb" sign on the door, and begun working. Suddenly, you hear a knock at the door. Instantly, you feel a rush of anger; your workflow has been disrupted. As you begrudgingly walk to the door, ready to unleash your frustration on whoever disturbed you, you find your neighbor standing there holding your wallet, which you dropped on the street and they were returning to you.

Instinctually, you had no way of knowing that this was someone doing you a favor; all you saw was an interruption to your project. If you had chosen to act on those instincts before gathering the necessary information to understand the nature of the intrusion, you would most likely have made a fool out of yourself.

While emotions are important and provide instinctual messages, they are not always accurate as they do not have all the information necessary before being triggered.

Having said that, each and every one of us is responsible for our actions, and our actions always have consequences as they affect the world around us.

Think of emotions as if they were like little storms inside our head that can make it hard to think straight.

You may find yourself in many situations where you must allow for these little storm to pass before taking an action, so that you may see the bigger picture under a clear blue sky.

Our emotions can also misinterpret a situation, such as feeling fear when watching a horror movie or being happy around someone who is not good for us. We can feel fear even though we are physically safe in a movie theater. We can feel joy when we receive a text from a person who has ghosted us for a week.

Making decisions while overwhelmed by emotions can hinder our ability to perceive a situation objectively. Emotions, much like animal instincts, are not necessarily rational.

While these responses are necessary when we find ourselves in a situation that requires a quick and immediate action, they may not be appropriate when we need to ensure that the decisions we make align with our best interests. It is wise to learn to take a step back, let the initial surge pass, ensure that the message sent by our emotions is correct (not a trigger), and that the information we have is complete before taking any action.

A Deeper Look at Dr. Ekman's Universal Emotions: Beyond "Positive" and "Negative"

While Dr. Paul Ekman identified seven basic universal emotions, labelling them simply as "positive" or "negative" can be reductive. Each emotion, including anger, joy, fear, sadness, disgust, surprise, and contempt, carries a complex interplay of biological, psychological, and social influences.

Anger

- Triggers: Frustration, threat, perceived injustice.

- Function: Motivates action to remove obstacles or achieve goals, can escalate to aggression if not managed constructively.

- Beyond the Label: Anger can be a signal of unmet needs, boundary violations, or a sense of powerlessness. Understanding the underlying cause can help you express anger assertively and productively.

Joy

- Triggers: Sensory experiences, witnessing kindness, personal achievements, beauty, connection.

- Function: Motivates approach behaviors, strengthens social bonds, promotes well-being.

- Beyond the Label: Joy is a multifaceted emotion encompassing happiness, contentment, and amusement. It fosters a sense of connection with oneself and the world, encouraging positive social interactions.

Fear

- Triggers: Real or imagined threats to physical, emotional, or psychological safety.

- Function: Signals danger and motivates protective behaviors like fight, flight, or freeze.

- Beyond the Label: Fear, while often associated with negativity, is a survival mechanism, keeping us cautious and alert in potentially harmful situations. However, it's important to distinguish healthy fear from debilitating anxiety.

Sadness

- Triggers: Loss of loved ones, endings, failure, disappointment.

- Function: Signals need for comfort and support, promotes healing and reflection.

- Beyond the Label: Sadness is a natural response to loss and disappointment, allowing us to process grief and eventually move forward. However, prolonged or intense sadness might indicate depression, or other issues requiring professional support.

Disgust

- Triggers: Bodily products, certain foods, rot/disease, injuries, perceived ugliness, immoral actions.

- Function: Protects from harmful substances and promotes hygiene. You can feel disgust around someone who is toxic to you.

- Beyond the Label: Beyond its evolutionary purpose of guiding us away from potential sources of contamination and disease, disgust also holds cultural variations in its triggers. While initially serving as a protective mechanism, this variation can lead to its misuse, promoting prejudice and discrimination.

Surprise

- Triggers: Sudden and unexpected occurrences.

- Function: Alerts us to potential danger or novelty, directs attention for further processing.

- Beyond the Label: Surprise, though brief, plays a crucial role in orienting ourselves to new situations. It promotes curiosity and exploration, encouraging us to learn and adapt to our environment.

Contempt

- Triggers: Perceived injustice, differences in social status, moral disapproval.

- Function: Signals dominance and asserts power over others.

- Beyond the Label: While contempt can stem from a sense of superiority, it can also be rooted in self-protection, frustration, hurt, and betrayal. Recognizing these underlying motivations is crucial for fostering healthy relationships and avoiding the detrimental consequences of contempt, such as communication breakdown and social isolation.

Secondary Emotions:

Emotions can become trapped in our bodies when not processed correctly. They can manifest in inappropriate ways and may be directed towards the wrong people or situations, often stemming from past traumas or unresolved experiences. Unprocessed emotions yearn to be acknowledged and understood. If left unaddressed, they may erupt in ways that are neither productive nor healthy.

This is why it's unhealthy to suppress how we feel. When emotions are suppressed, they become buried deep down inside and transform into something else that festers and distorts our perception of the world.

- Anxiety: A secondary emotion stemming from fear, often involving anticipation of potential future threats.
- Guilt: A blend of sadness and anger, arising from a sense of moral wrongdoing.
- Shame: A combination of sadness and disgust, linked to feelings of personal inadequacy or disgrace.
- Jealousy: A mix of sadness and anger, triggered by perceived threats to one's relationships or possessions.
- Envy: A blend of sadness and contempt, arising from the desire for what others possess.

Projections

Unprocessed emotions that remain unresolved can lead to a phenomenon known as projection, wherein one's internal state is projected onto their external environment. This implies that the emotions one is experiencing can influence how they perceive the people and things around them, essentially viewing the world through the lens of their mood.

For example, on a bad day, a painting may suddenly appear ugly, and the individual may feel the urge to tear it down. However, on a good day, they may look at the same painting and think to themselves, "How beautiful this piece of art is! How come I never noticed it before?"

On a bad day, one may find themselves easily irritated by minor issues, exhibiting a shorter temper, and harboring negative thoughts and feelings. Conversely, when feeling emotionally well, the tendency is to adopt a more positive outlook, displaying patience, understanding, and better interactions with others.

Projections can significantly influence a person's worldview, behavior, and actions, often causing harm to the people in their life and to themselves.

Processing Emotions

Recognize the Emotion

Recognizing the emotion is the first step in processing it. Take a moment to identify any physical sensations you may be experiencing and give the emotion a name, such as anger, sadness, or fear. This simple act of acknowledgment can help bring clarity and understanding to what you're feeling.

Allow Yourself to Feel the Emotion

It is important to allow yourself to feel the emotion, rather than trying to suppress it or push it away. This may involve taking deep breaths, and allowing yourself to feel the physical sensations associated with the emotion.

Reflect on the Cause of the Emotion

Pay attention to the now. If you feel fear, ask yourself is your life in danger at the moment? Or does the fear come from something deep within you? If you feel anger, ask yourself is it proportionate to the situation at hand? Or should you let it pass before you do or say anything? If you feel joy around a new encounter, ask yourself, is the person before you truly safe for you? Should you take it slow and get to know them better before revealing everything about yourself? Try to understand what triggered the emotion. Reflect on the events or thoughts that triggered your emotion. This can help you understand why you're feeling the way you do and what's behind the emotion.

Practice Mindfulness

Mindfulness is the practice of being present in the moment and observing your thoughts and feelings without judgment. This can help you gain perspective on the emotion and see it for what it is, rather than getting caught up in it.

Release the Emotion

Expressing your emotions in a healthy way is important. Name what you feel, talk about it, write about it, draw it out, or call a friend for support. Physical activities like running, dancing, or weightlifting can also help release pent-up emotions. However, it's important not to make significant decisions while experiencing intense emotions, as they may cloud judgment. It's best to wait for emotions to pass before making important decisions, ensuring clarity and rationality.

Feelings

Feelings are more complex and nuanced than emotions. They are influenced by a person's thoughts, beliefs, and memories. Feelings are long-lasting, and they can change over time. While emotions are an automatic response, feelings are the conscious experience of that response.

Feelings can be changed because our beliefs can change. For example, if we hold a belief that someone is bad for us, we may resent them. However, after practicing clear communication, we may change our beliefs and therefore our feelings towards that person may change as well. Once we clear a misunderstanding, we may begin to like a person that we previously disliked. We may fall out of love when we start to believe that a person is no longer good for us. We may stop feeling guilt and shame when we realize that what happened to us wasn't our fault. We may stop feeling inadequate in social situations when we gain self-esteem.

Recognizing Feelings Vs Emotions

- Emotions are often intense and short-lived, while feelings are more complex, nuanced, and are long-lasting.
- Emotions are automatic and instinctual, while feelings are influenced by a person's thoughts, beliefs, and memories.
- Emotions are physical and can be measured. Feelings are more of a mental process.
- Emotions are typically easier to identify because they are more intense and immediate, while feelings may be more subtle and take longer to recognize.
- Emotions are felt first, feelings are felt second.

A Story to Illustrate the Difference Between Feelings and Emotions

As you take a leisurely stroll through the forest, you unexpectedly come across a wild wolf. Your heart starts pounding and your body reacts on its own accord, causing you to scream and flee to safety. This is the natural response of fear to a perceived threat. Reflecting on the encounter later, you realize that the experience has left you with a dislike for wolves. Your feeling is based on the perception of your emotional response.

A week later, you have the opportunity to visit a wolf exhibit at a zoo. As you listen to a lecture about the importance of preserving wolves in their natural habitat, your perspective begins to shift and you gain a deeper understanding of these creatures. Despite this newfound knowledge, you still feel a sense of apprehension. The lecturer invites the audience to come closer and meet a tamed wolf. Your curiosity gets the better of you and you decide to take the opportunity. This decision is influenced by your previous experience, your memories and your newfound knowledge. As you approach the enclosure, the physical sensations of fear return - your heart races and your palms sweat. Fear is an automatic response, but you choose to push past it and pet the tamed wolf despite the physical sensation of fear being present in your body. As you make contact with the wolf, your feelings towards wolves change. Despite your instinctual fear of them, you now have a new found respect for them. Your feelings have evolved.

Journal Prompts

- Focusing within, how are you feeling right now?
- When you think about this week, which difficult feeling or emotion have you often tapped into and find most familiar (e.g., worry, guilt, exasperation, frustration, etc.)?
- How does that difficult emotion affect you physically?
- If you were to look more in-depth and beneath that feeling, what could you discover? (e.g., sad-

ness, disappointment, etc.)?
- If you were to set a small, achievable goal related to nurturing your emotional well-being, what might that look like for you?

The Lessons Learned

Self-control doesn't mean ignoring or suppressing your emotions. As a human being, it's natural to feel a range of emotions. The key to self-control is learning how to manage your reactions and responses when those emotions arise. We do this by acknowledging our emotions, giving ourselves permission to feel them, but also understanding that emotions are signals from our body. They are messages. You can receive the signal without necessarily acting on it immediately.

By validating what you are feeling, you are telling your body, "Ok, I got the message thanks." If you do not validate what you are feeling, your body will keep trying to send you the same message over and over again until you pay attention to it. You emotions want to be heard and acknowledged before they move on. They may become trapped in your body when they are repressed and ignored.

Think of handling your emotions in the same way that you would handle an unknown text message asking for your personal information. The first thing that you should do, before taking any action, is to verify the legitimacy and origin of the sender. Furthermore, if you ignore all the messages that you keep receiving, eventually, they will clog up your storage with useless data preventing your phone from receiving new and relevant messages. You must learn to differentiate the legitimate messages from the bad actors. Acknowledge that you received the message, either tag it as a spam and delete it permanently or save it. Leaving the message unread, does nothing but clog up your system.

By taking the time to critically assess the situation and evaluate your emotions, similarly to sorting the spam messages from the legitimate ones, you can ensure that you are making informed decisions rather than acting impulsively, and smashing a perfectly good phone for constantly freezing on you.

Chapter 9

Triggers

One of the significant triggers I had to work through in my healing process was a particular type of smile. This trigger stemmed from my upbringing and teenage years, during which I experienced panic attacks. Whenever I found myself in the throes of intense emotional distress, my mother would stand over me with a smile and dismissively call me an actress. She would mockingly remark, "Oh, look at this actress throwing a tantrum. How ridiculous." Then, she would proceed to shame and degrade me while I struggled to regain control over myself. This experience left me hypersensitive to anyone who looked at me with a half-smile for quite some time. I would immediately view it as mockery, going from 0 to 100, feeling absolutely certain about my interpretation of that smile, being unaware that this was a trigger. The irony wasn't lost on me—this behavior mirrored what my mother used to do, as she frequently attacked me for my natural resting face.

Another trigger for me became my own face. As an adult, I noticed that I had developed features resembling hers, particularly when I wore my hair in a certain way. This resemblance made it difficult for me to look at myself in the mirror for a long time, as I associated my appearance with her and the pain she caused. However, with time and understanding, I began to unravel the nature of my triggers and slowly work through them.

Triggers are created through painful life experiences and the perceptions that we hold about such experiences. They are indications of past unresolved pain and can creep up on you when you least expect them to.

"Being triggered" means that we suddenly re-experience the emotional sensations of a traumatic past event, as if it was happening all over again and project it onto our immediate environment. All it takes is a reminder which can be as subtle as a visual cue, a smell, a sound, an object, a facial expression, a song, even a conversation can be triggering. This subtle reminder acts as a time machine for our body and unknowingly brings us back in time.

The Nervous System

Survivors of narcissistic parenting do not face behavioral challenges in adulthood for "mysterious reasons", as the narcissistic family system is often quick to label the one who endured the worst treatment from the narcissistic parent.

These struggles have nothing to do with "inherent badness," "flaws," or "a deficient character"; rather, they are closely tied to how their nervous system has adapted to respond to their environment, essentially constituting trauma.

For scapegoated survivors, these struggles often begin during their formative years and persist into adulthood, as dysfunction becomes completely normalized in narcissistic family systems.

Lacking a dependable support system to turn to, our bodies instinctively swung between two extremes – gearing up to fight or flee when triggered, or succumbing to complacency and fearing assertiveness, avoidance, and panic over expressing an opinion.

The Autonomic Nervous System's Response to Stress

The autonomic nervous system (ANS) operates in two primary states: hyperarousal and hypoarousal. These states correspond to the body's Fight-Flight-Freeze-Fawn/Fold response, which helps us navigate various situations. Ideally, the ANS transitions between these states seamlessly based on the perceived threat level.

Consider a runner preparing for a race. They may experience hyperarousal just before the start, characterized by a heightened heart rate and increased alertness. Following the race, hypoarousal sets in, allowing them to breathe more easily and return their body to a resting and digestive state.

In situations of trauma, when a child is exposed to an antagonistic and unsafe caretaker while their nervous system is still developing, chronic exposure to threat can result in a state of hypervigilance. This means that their fight-or-flight response is consistently triggered.

When escape is not an option, the scapegoat may then enter a "freeze" state – the dorsal vagal state – representing a primitive emergency response. In this state, the fight-or-flight system may remain active while the body begins to shut down, leading to feelings of dissociation, numbness, and disconnection.

As a result, adult scapegoated survivors may experience dysregulation of these states. This means their nervous system might struggle to shift between hyperarousal and hypoarousal appropriately, leading to challenges in managing stress and emotions.

Signs of Hyperarousal:

- Physical symptoms: Increased heart rate, rapid breathing, sweating, muscle tension, dilated pupils, headaches, stomachaches, tremors (possible).
- Emotional symptoms: Anxiety, panic, irritabil-

ity, feeling overwhelmed, difficulty concentrating.
- Behavioral symptoms: Restlessness, fidgeting, pacing, difficulty sleeping, social withdrawal (in some cases of "freeze").

Signs of Hypoarousal:

- Physical symptoms: Slow heart rate, sluggishness, fatigue, shallow breathing, changes in sweating patterns, digestive issues.
- Emotional symptoms: Detachment, apathy, depression, difficulty feeling emotions, feelings of hopelessness.
- Behavioral symptoms: Difficulty concentrating, lack of motivation, social withdrawal, sleep problems (can include excessive sleeping in some cases).

Understanding these states is important in the context of trauma, as arousal and nervous dysregulation are symptoms of (C)PTSD (Complex Post-Traumatic Stress Disorder) and play a key role in how trauma impacts our lives. Childhood trauma, in particular, can disrupt the ability to shift healthily between arousal states, which are essential for maintaining both physical and psychological health. When our nervous system is unable to regulate itself, we become stuck in either hyperarousal or hypoarousal. When faced with challenging situations, we struggle to process the stress effectively. Additionally, it makes us more susceptible to re-traumatization when exposed to higher levels of stressors

The Amygdala Hijack

The "amygdala hijack" refers to a phenomenon where the amygdala, a part of the brain responsible for processing emotions, overrides the rational thinking processes of the prefrontal cortex during times of intense emotional arousal or stress. The amygdala is a part of the brain responsible for processing emotions, particularly fear and emotional memories. However, it doesn't have a sense of time, meaning it can react to any reminder of a painful memory as if they were immediate threats, even if they're not. When triggered, the amygdala initiates a fight, flight, or freeze response before the prefrontal cortex can fully process the situation. This can lead to impulsive reactions or behaviors driven by emotions rather than reasoned judgment.

The Elevator Shaft

Triggering can be thought of like an elevator shaft. The top floor is our very first reaction to the triggering event. Under this first reaction lies a second floor – a deeper, typically more vulnerable feeling. And beneath, there are several more floors, each with a deeper, less readily accessible emotional and/or physical feeling. Finally, we come to the basement, usually a core shock or wound often tracing all the way to our childhood. This core wound is so sensitive, so painful, so threatening, that we're desperate to avoid feeling it.

The stimulation of this wound helps cause the amygdala to interpret the trigger as a life and death situation and initiate a triggered response.

It is the core wound that drives the whole pattern of getting triggered.

Here's a typical example:

The trigger: Someone tells me I didn't do something right at work.
- 1st floor: Initial reaction (top floor): I feel defensive, insulted, attacked.
- 2nd floor down: A weak, sick feeling in my stomach. Feeling anxious, ruminating.
- 3rd floor down: If she's right, then I'm not good at what I do.
- 4th floor down: If I'm not good at what I do,

then I'm not worthy.
- 5th floor down: If I'm not worthy, then I'm not loveable.
- Basement (core wound): If I'm unlovable, then I'll be completely unloved and alone. It almost feels like, "What's the point in living?"

What Is State-Shifting?

State-shifting is the practice of learning to consciously shift our energy out of our triggered state and assisting our neo-cortex in re-establishing control. We aim to learn this skill so that we can respond appropriately to triggering situations.

The essence of the state-shifting practice lies in cultivating the discipline of refraining from acting when triggered, and then employing any one of a number of tools to bring ourselves back to a state of balance and inner clarity. This practice aids us in achieving better results and helps us avoid the collateral damage that often accompanies acting on our triggers.

There are four steps to the state-shifting practice:

- Step 1 Name it.
- Step 2 Take space appropriately.
- Step 3 Shift your state.
- Step 4 Deal with the situation.

Step 1. Name It.

The first step is to acknowledge and name when you're triggered. Recognize what is happening and consciously say to yourself, "I'm triggered."

Simply acknowledging that you're triggered doesn't immediately make it stop. The stress hormones will continue to surge through your body, and your emotions will remain inflamed. Nevertheless, the moment you consciously say, "I'm triggered," you awaken your adult self. It's as if a witness, an internal presence, has come forward that understands you're triggered.

To detect a trigger, pay attention to any sudden and overwhelming emotional responses that you may experience throughout the day. Look out for physical sensations such as a racing heart, sweating, shaking, or difficulty breathing. These can all be indicators that you are being triggered. Additionally, if you find yourself having an intense urge to fight, run, or feel frozen when there is no immediate danger, this could also be a sign that you are being triggered.

Possible Signs of Being Triggered

- Feeling powerless
- Feeling attacked
- Feeling judged
- Feeling unheard
- Feeling blamed
- Feeling disrespected
- Feeling lonely
- Feeling excluded
- Afraid to be honest
- Feeling forgotten
- Feeling manipulated
- Feeling controlled
- Feeling trapped
- Feeling unsafe
- Feeling disconnected
- Feeling avoidant
- Feeling angry
- Feeling unloved
- Running away

It is completely normal to experience any of the aforementioned feelings when in an unsafe situation. However, these emotions can also frequently arise at the slightest reminders of our past. It's important to recognize that we can't always avoid feeling triggered in the moment; nevertheless, we can learn to identify when we're being triggered. This awareness can help us refrain from projecting our issues onto people who had nothing to do with our difficult upbringing.

While communication is vital, it's essential to remember that others are not responsible for maintaining our calmness. While we can express what we're going through, we need to manage our expectations regarding how much others can support us. Expecting people to tread carefully around our triggers or becoming upset with them for triggering us only perpetuates trauma. Instead, we must fiercely protect our loved ones from ever experiencing what we endured and become a shield that halts this negative energy from spreading further.

Some Trigger examples:

- A girl who has been given the silent treatment by a parent as a child might panic at an unanswered text and abruptly end the relationship without getting the facts first. The unanswered test brought her back to the trauma of parental emotional abuse.

- A husband who grew up in a raging home avoids important conversations with his wife that are necessary for the growth of the relationship "If we don't talk about it, the problem doesn't exist"' His subconscious belief that disagreements equate rage, triggers the flight response when confronted with an issue.

- A scapegoat who has been chronically invalidated by their family, might be triggered by another person accidentally being distracted during a conversation as it reminds them of the past experiences of not being heard and understood, which could falsely lead to feeling unimportant and not valued.

Step 2. Take Space Appropriately.

The key to state-shifting is to remember: Do not obey the trigger. Once you've been able to name It, the

critical next step in state-shifting is to take space appropriately from the triggering situation. There are two reasons:
1. If you stay in the situation, you will keep getting retriggered.
2. If you stay in the situation, you are likely to say or do something you will later regret.

Here are some examples of how to appropriately take space in different situations:

Direct approaches:

- Communicate your need for space: "I'm feeling a bit reactive/unclear/emotional. I could really use some time to gather my thoughts. How about we continue this conversation later?"
- Agree to disagree and suggest resuming later: "Let's leave it at that for now. I need some time to process my thoughts."

Indirect approaches:

- Use a bathroom break or phone distraction: Excuse yourself by saying, "I need to use the bathroom," or take out your phone and say, "Sorry, I have to respond to this message. It's urgent." These universally recognized opportunities can provide you with personal space.

- Buy yourself time with a neutral response: If someone says something triggering, respond with an open-ended comment to give yourself a moment to collect your thoughts. For example, you can say, "Interesting" or "That's one way of looking at it."

It may be inadvisable to say "I'm triggered" to someone who isn't a trusted source of support due to the following reasons:

1. Not everyone may be familiar with the concept of trauma triggers, and how it affects you. Sharing

that you are triggered without providing further context or explanation may confuse or leave the other person unsure of how to respond appropriately.

2. While sharing your triggers can be helpful in certain supportive relationships or therapeutic settings, not everyone may be equipped or willing to provide the support and understanding you need. Some could potentially have dismissive or invalidating reactions, adding to your distress.

There can be challenges to taking space appropriately, but when you really understand that learning to manage your trigger completely depends on your taking the space you need, you can usually find a way to do it.

However, When physical space is not easily accessible, it can still be helpful to create some psychological space. You can achieve this by temporarily disengaging from the discussion.

It's important to note that taking space appropriately doesn't mean avoiding or ignoring the triggering situation. It simply provides a momentary respite to collect yourself and regroup. Remember that state shifting is not avoidance.

Once you have stepped away from the triggering situation, you can move on to Step 3, which focuses on shifting your state of being and finding a way to return to a more balanced and rational mindset.

Step 3. Shift Your State

Once we are no longer actively provoked by the trigger, the flight/fight response will usually subside gradually. But, it can take a while.

Recovery time is impacted by:
- The intensity of the trigger and the degree of emotional reaction and/or neurological trauma.
- How quickly you remove yourself from the triggering situation.

- Your general state of mind/body wellness. We're more susceptible to being triggered when we're overtired, have low blood sugar, etc..

Things that you can do:

Breathe

When we're triggered, we typically start either holding our breath or hyperventilating. Carbon dioxide builds up, creating that panicky feeling akin to when we've been underwater too long. The simplest state-shifting tool is to begin taking deep breaths, thereby increasing the amount of oxygen entering our lungs. Simple but effective—especially if we catch our triggering early before we spiral out of control.

Move energy

One of the most powerful and quickest methods to shift out of a triggered state is to participate in vigorous physical exercise. This can include activities such as dancing, jogging, working out, biking – anything that gets the heart pumping. Additionally, using our voice, such as singing, can also be beneficial. The goal is to increase oxygen flow, expend excess energy generated by the fight/flight response, and release endorphins that promote feelings of well-being.

Feel your feelings

Nature has provided us with a simple and effective method for dealing with emotions. Sometimes, when we've been triggered, what we actually need is to allow ourselves to feel, especially the deeper emotions that lie underneath our initial reactions, and simply cry it out.

Meditation/prayer

Mediation, prayer, chanting, and other forms of spiritual practice are all powerful tools for shifting our state. They are highly effective, having been field-tested for thousands of years. However, it helps to have developed a foundational practice before you try to make use of these in a triggered situation.

Change your physical environment

This remarkably simple maneuver can be surprisingly effective: change your physical environment. Go to a different room. Even better—if you can manage it, go outside.

Anchoring

Anchoring is a powerful psychological technique used to associate a particular state of mind, emotion, or behavior with a specific trigger or stimulus (like an object, image, gesture, smell etc). By creating anchors, you can intentionally access desired emotional states or behaviors when needed, providing a sense of control and empowerment in various situations. Here's how you can create your own anchors:

- Identify Your Safety Zone: Begin by reflecting on situations, environments, or experiences where you feel most safe, calm, and grounded. This could be a physical space, such as your bedroom or a quiet corner in nature, or it could be an activity that brings you comfort, like listening to calming music or practicing deep breathing exercises. Alternatively, your safety zone could be a mental space or a part of your body that feels safe or neutral, such as your fingers or feet. Understanding what constitutes your safety zone is important for creating effective anchors that can help you access this state of calm and security when needed.

- Choose a Positive Trigger: Once you've identified your safety zone, select a specific trigger or stimulus that you can use to anchor this feeling of safety and calmness. This trigger could be a physical gesture, such as pressing your thumb and forefinger together, or a visual cue, such as focusing on a particular object or image. It's important to choose a trigger that is easy to access and inconspicuous, allowing you to use it discreetly in various situations.

- Associate the Trigger: With your trigger selected, intentionally associate it with the feeling of safety and calmness from your identified safety zone. Spend some time in your safety zone, fully immersing yourself in the feelings of comfort and security. As you experience these emotions, engage with your chosen trigger, repeating the process multiple times to strengthen the association between the trigger and the desired emotional state.

- Practice Consistently: Like any skill, anchoring requires consistent practice to become effective. Set aside time each day to practice activating your anchor and accessing the associated state of mind or emotion. Start by practicing in low-stress situations where you can focus on refining your technique, gradually progressing to more challenging scenarios as you build confidence in your ability to anchor your desired state.

- Apply in Real-Life Situations: Once you feel comfortable with your anchor, begin incorporating it into real-life situations where you could benefit from accessing your desired emotional state.

Choose cues that can quickly bring you back to your power zone. These can be:
- Physical Anchor: Find a strong, confident body posture that embodies your power zone. Feel your feet grounded and your core engaged.
- Visual Anchor: Select a powerful image that resonates with you. This could be a natural element

like a river or a mountain, a revered person, or a spiritual symbol. When triggered, vividly imagine this image and feel the associated strength flowing into you.
- Auditory Anchor: Create a short, empowering phrase or mantra that resonates with your sense of inner strength. Examples include "This will pass," "I am enough," or "I am a survivor." Repeat this phrase silently or internally when triggered to evoke feelings of calm and power.

Step 4. Decide How to Deal with the Situation.

After the trigger has passed, it's important to revisit the situation and address it if necessary, particularly if the person who triggered you is someone with whom you have a significant ongoing relationship. Take a moment to consider whether it's worth expending your energy on addressing the issue. For example:

1. If the person's behavior towards you is disrespectful, decrease the amount of time you spend with them. Practice the "gray rock" technique and avoid personal conversations. Keep the interaction platonic. Remember, you are not obligated to maintain a relationship with anyone, and sometimes it's best to go low or no contact to prioritize your mental health.

2. View this situation as a learning experience that allows you to strengthen yourself. Practice your communication skills to gain clarity. Keep in mind that the reality may be different from what you initially perceived.

Respecting Your Window of Tolerance

Respecting your Window of Tolerance is imperative for maintaining emotional balance and well-being. You can imagine your emotional state as being a dial with an ideal setting – your Window of Tolerance – where your nervous system feels comfortable and controlled. Within this zone, you feel safe, enabling you to function optimally. You communicate effectively, form meaningful connections, and tackle challenges constructively.

However, when stressors escalate, the dial turns up too high, triggering the "fight, flight, or freeze" response. While this survival mechanism is innate, it inhibits clear communication and problem-solving. Critical thinking is impaired, making it challenging to find long-term solutions.

Respecting your Window of Tolerance is not only vital for your relationships but also for your personal well-being. You are not obligated to remain in triggering situations, and prioritizing your body, mind, and soul is paramount. When you are calm and composed, you can listen attentively, articulate your thoughts clearly, and navigate disagreements healthily.

By staying within your emotional sweet spot, you create an optimal environment for genuine connection and effective communication. Therefore, be mindful of your emotional states as you work towards healing your nervous system. Recognizing and honoring your Window of Tolerance fosters resilience, promotes self-care, and paves the way for meaningful growth and healing.

Journal Prompts

- Think about a specific situation or event that led to a strong emotional response. What were the circumstances leading up to the event, and what were your thoughts and feelings at the time?
- Reflect on patterns in your life that consistently lead to negative emotional responses. What are the common themes or triggers in these situations?
- Consider a time when you felt triggered by a

seemingly insignificant event. What were the underlying emotions or memories that were stirred up by this trigger?
- What are some physical sensations or symptoms that you experience when you are triggered? How do these sensations contribute to your emotional response?
- Think about a specific relationship or interaction that consistently triggers negative emotions. What are the specific actions or behaviors of the other person that trigger these emotions?

The Lessons Learned

Triggers are your body's attempt to safeguard you, and it is perfectly acceptable to take time for yourself to allow the triggers to dissipate. It's important to recognize that you have endured a great deal, and you must allocate the time necessary for your recovery. You do not have to remain in situations that trigger you, and it's essential to prioritize your mental health without feeling any remorse for taking the necessary steps to keep yourself secure.

Having said that, it is important to remember that our perceptions act as a target, and triggers have a way of honing in and attaching themselves to external objects or people, leading to intense reactions that are often disproportionate or inappropriate for the circumstance. Essentially, triggers act as powerful projections that can obstruct our ability to see alternative perspectives. They can cause us to re-experience the past, making it feel like the present.

While our perceptions give our life meaning and direction, they also act as blockers to the unknown. Once we become set in our ways, it become harder to change. Be aware of this as you focus on your healing and personal growth.

Being in sync with the present means being aware of and open to new perspectives and experiences. It means not allowing our past experiences and perceptions to blind us to new possibilities and opportunities. It requires being mindful of our assumptions and being willing to question them. It also means being willing to listen and consider different viewpoints, rather than jumping to conclusions. In this way, we can expand our understanding of the world and ourselves, and live in a more open, authentic, and meaningful way.

Chapter 10

Affect of Abandonment Fears

The fear of abandonment had a profound impact on my life, leading to ongoing struggles and preventing me from finding fulfillment for a significant period of time. Whenever I sensed disapproval or the possibility of disappointing someone, it triggered extreme avoidance behaviors in me. This pattern affected various aspects of my life, both personally and professionally. In an effort to protect myself, I would often push others away preemptively, fearing rejection or abandonment. This made it difficult for me to form and maintain healthy relationships. Conversely, I also experienced intense attachment to certain people, fearing their loss so intensely that I suffocated them with my neediness. This constant oscillation between extremes left me unable to find a balanced approach to relationships.

I had a deep-seated belief that love was a scarce resource, and if attention was given elsewhere, there wouldn't be any love left for me. This struggle to maintain a healthy balance in my relationships drew the wrong kind of people into my life and pushed away those who were genuinely healthy for me.

Confronting the reality of my true self and acknowledging the consequences of my actions was an arduous and gradual process, demanding me to confront profound underlying issues. It was essential for me to confront the core of my fears to reclaim control of my life, advance my personal growth, and cultivate self-improvement.

About Fear

Fear, a primal emotion, serves a vital purpose as our body's built-in alarm system. It helps us identify potential dangers in our environment and triggers our fight-or-flight response to evade danger as quickly as possible.

There are two main types of fear. The first is logical fear, a rational response to an immediate threat, such as a fire or a wild animal. This type of fear is essential for survival, prompting us to take swift action to protect ourselves.

The second type of fear is triggered not by immediate dangers, but by memories, experiences, or imagined scenarios. This type of fear, also called emotional or learned fear, can be far more disruptive. It can range from mild anxieties to debilitating phobias, leading to excessive worry, crippling anxieties, and avoidance behaviors that limit our lives.

Some examples of emotional fear include:

- Social Situations: Fear of public speaking, social gatherings, or public scrutiny, even though there's no real threat of harm. This could stem from past negative experiences or a fear of being judged.

- Specific Phobias: Fear of heights, spiders, enclosed spaces, or flying, even though the actual danger might be minimal. These phobias can be triggered by past experiences or learned associations.

- Performance Anxiety: Fear of failure or embarrassment when performing a task, like playing a sport or giving a presentation. This can lead to avoidance or hinder performance, even though the consequences of failure might not be severe.

- Abandonment Fear: This fear can stem from the experience of being emotionally neglected, criticized, or blamed by caregivers. This can lead to a deep-seated belief that one is unlovable or unworthy, making them hypervigilant to signs of potential rejection or abandonment, especially in situations reminiscent of past experiences.

Exploring Your Attachment Style

The wounds of rejection and disdain can leave deep scars, shaping how we see ourselves and navigate relationships. Early experiences can make it challenging to find self-validation, trust others, and manage emotions – all remnants of a toxic family dynamic.

Becoming mindful of your attachment style is a powerful initial step you can take toward healing. It involves recognizing that the way you connect with others may carry imprints from your past experiences. This awareness is pivotal because it lays the groundwork for breaking free from ingrained relationship patterns established during your tumultuous upbringing. Understanding your attachment style acts as a spotlight in the shadows, illuminating reasons behind trust issues or discomfort with intimacy.

Attachment styles, categorized as secure, anxious, avoidant, and disorganized, reflect various patterns of relating.

Secure Attachment

Consistent and Responsive Caregivers.

- Emotional availability: Caregivers were attuned to the child's needs and emotions, responding warmly and promptly.
- Predictability and reliability: Caregivers provided consistent routines and boundaries, creating a sense of security and trust in the environment.
- Positive regard: Caregivers expressed love, acceptance, and validation, fostering a healthy self-esteem in the child.
- Empathy and support: Caregivers acknowledged and validated the child's feelings, providing comfort and guidance during difficult moments.

Outcome:

- High self-esteem: Individuals feel confident and worthy, believing in their own abilities and value.
- Positive self-perception: They view themselves favorably, acknowledging both strengths and weaknesses with self-compassion.
- Healthy autonomy: They feel comfortable exploring the world independently, knowing they have a secure base to return to.
- Trust in others: They believe others are generally reliable and trustworthy, allowing them to form open and genuine relationships.

Anxious Attachment

Inconsistent, unpredictable, or emotionally dysregulated caregivers.

While inconsistency and unpredictability in caregiving are key factors, there are different subtypes of anxious attachment with nuanced variations.

- Preoccupied/Anxious-Ambivalent: Intense de-

sire for closeness and intimacy intertwined with fear of abandonment, leading to clinginess, jealousy, and emotional highs and lows.
- Fearful-Avoidant: Desire for intimacy mixed with fear of emotional vulnerability, resulting in push-pull dynamics and difficulty maintaining long-term relationships.

Outcome:

Both subtypes share core anxious attachment outcomes:
- Fear of abandonment: This is a constant worry, triggering intense anxiety and insecurity at potential signs of rejection or distance.
- Need for reassurance: Individuals seek constant validation and approval from others, often struggling to believe in their own worth.
- Hypervigilance: They are overly sensitive to perceived threats or slights, misinterpreting neutral actions as negativity.
- Difficulty with trust: Building trust in others is challenging due to past experiences of inconsistency and betrayal.
- Emotional dysregulation: Difficulty managing emotions can lead to overreactions, mood swings, and difficulty communicating effectively.

Avoidant Attachment

Emotionally distant or unavailable caregivers.

- Discomfort with intimacy: Emotional closeness and vulnerability trigger discomfort, leading to emotional distancing and resistance to commitment.
- Self-sufficiency: They focus on independence and self-reliance, fearing dependence on others and potential emotional pain.
- Suppressing emotions: Difficulty expressing and acknowledging emotions, both positive and neg-

ative, leading to emotional unavailability.
- Fear of rejection: Underlying fear of emotional vulnerability and intimacy hides behind a facade of indifference or disinterest.
- Pushing others away: Subtly or directly distancing themselves from others before getting too close, preventing deeper connections.

Outcome:

- Isolation and loneliness: Difficulty forming deep connections leaves individuals feeling emotionally isolated and potentially lonely.
- Fear of intimacy: Sabotaging potential relationships before experiencing vulnerability and emotional intimacy.
- Intimacy deprivation: Missing out on the fulfillment and joy that comes from deep and meaningful connections.
- Emotional suppression: Can lead to difficulty managing emotions effectively, impacting well-being and mental health.
- Conflict avoidance: Difficulty addressing problems or navigating conflict in relationships can lead to unhealthy patterns.

Disorganized Attachment

Traumatic experiences with caregivers where fear, inconsistency, and unpredictability were intertwined.

- Conflicting desires: Intense desire for closeness and love juxtaposed with a deep fear of intimacy and betrayal, leading to confusing and unstable attachment behaviors.
- Unpredictable reactions: Difficulty regulating emotions and responding erratically to perceived threats or abandonment cues.
- Dissociation: Disconnecting from self or surroundings as a coping mechanism during over-

whelming emotions.
- Internalized chaos: Reflecting the inconsistent caregiving environment, individuals experience internal confusion and conflicting beliefs about themselves and others.
- Difficulty trusting others: Deep fear of betrayal makes trusting others incredibly challenging, even when desiring connection.

Outcome:

- Unstable relationships: Characterized by intense highs and lows, fear of abandonment, and difficulty maintaining healthy boundaries.
- Identity issues: Confusion about self-worth and identity due to contradictory messages received from caregivers.
- Self-harm or risky behaviors: Attempts to regulate overwhelming emotions or gain control in unpredictable environments.
- Mental health challenges: Increased risk of depression, anxiety, post-traumatic stress disorder (PTSD), and borderline personality disorder (BPD).

Understanding your attachment style can be a powerful tool for personal growth and emotional healing. While discovering your attachment style may initially reveal patterns and behaviors that seem limiting or challenging, it's important to recognize that this knowledge doesn't define you indefinitely. Instead, it provides a roadmap for self-awareness and the opportunity for positive change.

Through mindfulness, you can observe how your attachment style influences your interactions and choices in real-time. For example, you may notice moments of anxiety or avoidance arising in relationships and learn to respond with greater understanding and compassion. Instead of reacting impulsively based on past conditioning, mindfulness empowers you to pause, reflect, and consciously choose how to engage with others.

Pushing Beyond the Fear

The Power of Saying No

The fear of abandonment can lead us to prioritize others' needs over our own, often without realizing the cost to ourselves.

When we say yes to something we should say no to, we're agreeing to invest our energy, time, and resources, often at the expense of our well-being.

Saying yes when we should say no means sacrificing a part of ourselves, potentially causing discomfort, depleting our resources, and straining our mental health, all to maintain a connection with someone who may not reciprocate our efforts.

Each time we overcommit, we chip away at our essence, leaving ourselves feeling empty and drained. The lingering question becomes: how do we fill the void we've created?

Unfortunately, the answer may be that we can't. When we give beyond our means, we're left with nothing for ourselves. Sacrificing our peace and well-being for others' approval or to maintain relationships can have long-lasting effects on our mental health.

Meanwhile, the recipients of our generosity may not fully appreciate or understand our capacity or the impact of their requests. They may be focused on their own needs, unaware or indifferent to the toll it takes on us.

Ultimately, we must prioritize our own well-being and not rely on others to do so for us. We are our own safety net, and sacrificing our needs for the sake of others is a risky bet that often leaves us unsupported.

Sacrificing ourselves, not out of a sense of healthy responsibility as a parent would for a child, but out of fear of being abandoned, will inevitably lead to living a life filed with resentment, frustrations and anger.

We may believe that because we sacrificed ourselves to fulfill another person's needs, they will surely love us back or reciprocate when our resources are low and theirs are plentiful. This is a false belief.

With this kind of mindset, you must prepare to have your heart broken again and again.

True love and healthy relationships are built on mutual respect, trust, and understanding of each other's needs and boundaries. Self-sacrifice is not a normal everyday relationship requirement between two capable adults.

This unhealthy sacrificial mindset has been taught to us by our dysfunctional family system, where boundaries were not respected, and the needs of one member were prioritized over the needs of others. This can lead to a pattern of codependency, where we believe that we need to sacrifice ourselves in order to gain love and acceptance from others.

Covert abuse conditions us to believe that we are not enough just as we are, that we are unworthy of unconditional love unless we bend over backwards, and that we should sacrifice our needs while simultaneously elevating the needs of the other person above anything and everything, in the name of love. It is important to recognize and break this cycle, and to learn to create healthy relationships based on mutual respect, trust, and understanding of each other's needs and boundaries.

Going beyond our limits for someone will not bind that person to us, nor will it prevent abandonment.

Not only is this type of mindset unhealthy for our mental health, it also attracts all sorts of opportunistic manipulators and users into our lives.

Furthermore, your inability to say no may backfire and push healthy friends away. You may begin to feel resentment towards people who set healthy boundaries for themselves and this feeling may cause you to inadvertently sabotage a good friendship.

When a person sets boundaries and communicates their limits, it can be easy for us to misinterpret this as selfish behavior, especially if we are used to going beyond our limits and draining our own resources for everyone. We may feel heartbreak or even betrayal to hear someone else say no, while in reality they are simply taking care of themselves, which is a crucial aspect of any healthy relationship. A good friend will respect your limits and a healthy "no" is to be expected both ways in a healthy friendship every once in a while.

Love is not about sacrificing your needs, but about nurturing them. Setting boundaries and communicating our needs is an essential part of any healthy relationship. Saying no is not selfish, it is a necessary and healthy aspect of self-care. It is important to recognize the difference between a healthy yes and a fear based one, and to create a balance where both parties can feel respected, heard and loved even when the answer is the occasional no.

Maintaining a balance between caring for others and taking care of ourselves will avoid feelings of resentment and unrealistic expectations of others.

A person who is healthy for you, will never abandon you for saying no.

What's the Worse That Can Happen?

When dealing with abandonment fears, it can be easy to imagine the worst possible scenarios and become overwhelmed by feelings of anxiety and insecurity. Asking yourself "what is the absolute worst that can happen?" and preparing a strategy to accept it, can help to reduce the impact of these fears and improve your emotional well-being.

For example, if you have a fear of being abandoned by a romantic partner, the worst-case scenario might be that they do in fact leave you. To prepare for this possibility, you can develop a plan to take care of yourself emotionally and financially. You may then relax and enjoy the ride and see where it may lead you knowing that you can always fall back on yourself if it doesn't work out.

Another example is if you fear being abandoned by friends, the worst-case scenario might be that they do in fact stop talking to you. To prepare for this possibility, you can focus on a hobby, activities that make you happy, self-care and self-compassion as a way to take care of yourself emotionally. This in fact, will make your life richer, and you will feel more comfortable with your interactions knowing that your entire world doesn't revolve around a particular group of people.

Preparing for the worst-case scenario does not mean that it will happen, but it can help you to feel more in control of the situation and reduce feelings of anxiety and insecurity. It is a way of being realistic and at the same time preparing for the worst so it doesn't catch you off guard.

Being prepared for the worst-case scenario does not mean that you have to accept it as inevitable. Be present with the people in your life, practice your communications skills, lay down healthy boundaries and see what happens. You can do all of this comfortably knowing that you have your own back no matter what happens.

Letting Go

Let them focus on you when they want to, and because they want to. Not because they have to, because you made them, or because you went out of your way to get their attention.

When dealing with fears of abandonment, it can be easy to fall into the trap of trying to control others in order to feel secure in our relationships. We may try to control how others think, feel, and act in order to prevent them from leaving us.

However, trying to control others is not only unhealthy for our relationships, but it also prevents us from truly healing and addressing our fears of abandonment. When we keep a tight grip on another, we are not facing our own fears and insecurities. We are not learning to trust ourselves and our own abilities to handle any potential rejection or abandonment. We are not addressing the real issue. We are only projecting our issues and insecurities onto them. This is not peaceful living for either party.

It's important to remember that every person is autonomous and has their own agency. We cannot control their thoughts, feelings, or actions. We can only control our own thoughts, feelings, and actions. By focusing on taking care of ourselves and learning to trust ourselves, we can build a strong foundation of self-worth and self-love that will be the foundation of a healthy and fulfilling life.

Additionally, holding on too tight may cause them to feel resentful and trapped in the relationship, and they may ultimately leave the relationship. It's much more important to focus on building healthy and mutual relationships, where both parties feel free to express themselves, and respect each other's boundaries and limits.

Love is not a competition and there is always enough to go around. The more freedom a person has to be themselves, pursue their interests, and live their life as they please, the more authentic the love they have for others will be.

Trust and growth are important components of any healthy relationship and cannot be achieved if one person is constantly holding on too tightly.

When you let go, you open up space for growth and development. By allowing others to make their own choices and decisions, you plant the seeds of trust that can grow and strengthen as the relationship evolves. While it is possible for relationships to falter, it is not fair to hold someone accountable for something they have not yet done. Give them the opportunity to demonstrate their character and intentions. If the relationship does not work out, you will be fine and you will move on. But if it does, the trust cultivated can become an unbreakable bond.

Pay Less Attention to Others, and More Attention to You

Turn the focus away from other people and instead focus on building your own self-esteem. When your self-worth is based on the validation and acceptance of others, you may experience feelings of worthlessness, insecurity and your abandonment fears are amplified. When you have low self-esteem, you believe you are not worthy of love and respect.

However, by shifting the focus to yourself and working on building your self-esteem, you can learn to value and accept yourself regardless of the presence or absence of a relationship. This can involve setting personal goals, focusing on a passion or hobby, practicing self-care and self-compassion, developing a sense of purpose and more importantly making decisions that empower you.

By working on your own self-esteem, you can learn to trust in your own abilities and worth, rather than relying on the validation of others. This can help to alleviate fears of abandonment and provide a sense of security in your own self. Remember that you are in charge of your own happiness and self-worth, and that you don't need anyone else to validate you to be worth something.

Journal Prompts

- Reflect on past experiences of abandonment and identify the strengths and qualities that helped you to overcome them. How can you tap into these strengths in future situations?
- Think about the people in your life who have been supportive and consistent. How have they helped to improve your feelings of self-worth and security in relationships?
- What are some self-care practices that you can implement to help build resilience against feel-

ings of abandonment?
- Consider the ways in which you have grown and changed as a result of past experiences of abandonment. How can you use this growth to build a more positive and fulfilling future?
- Think about the things you value most in yourself and your life. How can you use these values to guide your decisions and actions to improve your self-esteem and reduce abandonment fears?
- What are some positive affirmations or personal mantras that you can use to remind yourself of your own worth and strength when feeling vulnerable to abandonment?

The Lessons Learned

Remember this, plain and simple: you deserve respect and dignity. It's not a privilege, it's a basic right.

- Your past doesn't dictate your present or future. Every day is a fresh start, a chance to shape your own story.

- Not everyone will like you, and that's okay. Don't twist yourself into knots trying to win everyone's approval. It's impossible, and it's not worth it.

- Don't sacrifice your well-being for the sake of others. Your needs matter, and it's okay to prioritize them.

- You're not defined by what others think of you. Their opinions don't determine your worth.

- Set boundaries and stick to them. Say no when you need to, without guilt.

- Never beg for a relationships or validation.

- Stay true to your values, even if it means not everyone will like you. It's better to be true to yourself than to betray what you believe in.

- And remember, if someone doesn't respect you, they don't deserve a place in your life. Walk away and don't look back.

Remember that you are enough.

Chapter 11
Affect of Guilt

The idea of loved ones feeling betrayed by your decision to protect yourself is dreadful. You may feel guilty about leaving behind enablers who despite enabling the narcissist have also shown you kindness in private. Doubts may creep in, causing you to question if leaving the family system was the right decision, and whether you are the traitor they think you are.

Toxic guilt can be a formidable and self-destructive obstacle. It often serves as the main driving force that prevents many of us from leaving toxic environments.

Guilt has led us scapegoats to bear burdens that we should never have carried, and that were never our responsibility to carry in the first place. It is a weapon used by narcissists to exert control, and it can be one of the greatest vulnerabilities for the scapegoat who grows up in such family dynamics.

It's important to recognize that the feelings of guilt you experience are not based on reality, but are a result of manipulation and abuse from the narcissistic family system. To gain clarity, take a step back and observe the situation objectively without letting guilt cloud your judgment.

Upon closer examination, you'll notice that the mentality of "one for all and all for one" takes precedence over any care or concern for your emotional well-being. The invalidation of your experiences, the minimizing of inappropriate behavior, and the unrealistic expectations of loyalty and devotion to someone who is the source of your pain and trauma are all part of the system in which you were raised.

Remember that you are not the traitor that they claim you are. It is in fact the other way around. They betrayed you, just like my father betrayed me again and again and again. Unfortunately guilt rendered me unable to see it at the time.

Taking steps to protect yourself from the harm that the narcissistic family system inflicts does not make you a terrible person. It's okay to prioritize your own well-being and to distance yourself from those who are not capable of showing you empathy and respect.

Their refusal to validate your struggles and use of guilt to keep you from leaving has played a massive role in enabling the narcissist's hold over you. The people who trigger your guilt are a part of a dysfunctional system that perpetuates the same cycle of abuse. Despite witnessing your pain and suffering, they choose to deny your reality, and the cycle continues to repeat itself with the unappeasable narcissist at the center.

They chose not to validate your struggles, because they, and the narcissist, are in the same team. They operate as one. You are not dealing with one person, you are dealing with a system that has been created to keep dysfunction going.

It is not healthy or normal for a family to require that everyone have the same relationship with one specific member, especially when that member is toxic. It is healthy to question why your loved ones cannot have a healthy relationship with you independent from the relationship with the narcissist. It is also healthy to question if they see the harm that this dynamic is causing you and if they hold the same empathy and regard for you as they do for the narcissist.

The narcissist forces all family members to choose sides, and this is a common tactic used by narcissist to maintain control over their family members. There will never be a middle ground.

In a healthy family, there is enough love, empathy and validation to go around, but in a narcissistic family system, family members must compete for these things. In a narcissistic family system, there are winners and losers; the chosen "devils" and the chosen "angels". At the end of the day, hope can be a losing game for the scapegoat.

Guilt Manifestations

Guilt can be a heavy burden, manifesting not just emotionally but physically as well. Some people experience a tightness or heaviness in their chest, stomach, or throat. This physical discomfort can be accompanied by fatigue or changes in appetite.

Emotionally, guilt can be a relentless critic. It chips away at your self-esteem, leaving you doubting yourself and filled with regret for your actions (or inactions). You might find yourself replaying the situation in your mind, haunted by thoughts like "I should have known better" or "I can't believe I did that." The constant barrage of negativity can be overwhelming, making it difficult to focus on anything else.

This all-encompassing guilt can feel like it takes up a significant amount of mental space, leaving little room for other thoughts or emotions. It becomes a loop that's hard to escape, hindering your ability to move forward.

Sometimes feeling a dose of guilt is healthy, and sometimes it is not.

Narcissists rarely apologize or take responsibility for their actions. This lack of guilt stems from an inflated sense of self-importance and a lack of empathy. They struggle to see how their actions negatively affect others, believing their feelings and experiences are morally superior. This distorted self-perception leaves them entitled to lash out at those closest to them, creating a confusing and emotionally volatile environment. The absence of guilt makes positive change difficult, leaving their targets feeling hurt, confused, and perpetually on edge.

Feeling guilty can serve as a valuable teacher, especially when it arises from realizing that one's actions have caused harm to another person.

However, it's important to differentiate this healthy guilt from the toxic guilt that is imposed on the scapegoat in a narcissistic family system, which is not based on reality.

For us scapegoats, such a distinction may be very difficult to make, because our narcissistic parent taught us that we cause harm when we set down boundaries, when we communicate our limits, when we attend to our needs, when we express emotions, feelings, and opinions that differ from theirs. The list of ways that a scapegoat is made to feel guilty in a narcissistic family system is endless, and the distinction between healthy guilt and toxic guilt becomes blurred.

Recognizing Toxic Guilt Vs Healthy Guilt

The Source

Healthy guilt is typically a result of actions or behaviors that were genuinely harmful or hurtful to others, whereas toxic guilt is often imposed by others or is the result of internalized negative beliefs.

The Feeling

Healthy guilt is a feeling of remorse or regret that can motivate a person to make amends or change their behavior, while toxic guilt is a heavy, overwhelming feeling that can lead to feelings of worthlessness and self-criticism.

The Duration

Healthy guilt is usually short-lived and is resolved when the person takes appropriate action to make amends, while toxic guilt can linger and fester for long periods of time.

The Response

Healthy guilt often leads to taking responsibility and making amends, while toxic guilt can lead to procrastination, avoidance, or self-criticism. Toxic guilt doesn't permit you to have limits.

The Perspective

Healthy guilt is often a reminder that one's actions have consequences and it helps to develop empathy and consideration for others, whereas toxic guilt can lead to a distorted self-perception, where one sees oneself as inherently flawed or bad.

The Proportionality

Healthy guilt is a proportionate response to the action taken, whereas toxic guilt often leads to excessive self-blame and negative self-talk.

The Self-Compassion

Healthy guilt is often accompanied by self-compassion, where one is kind and understanding towards oneself, whereas toxic guilt is often accompanied by self-judgment and self-criticism.

Toxic Empathy

Toxic empathy refers to an excessive and unhealthy form of empathy that causes us to lose sight of our own needs and boundaries. It often manifests as feeling responsible for another person's emotions or problems, and becoming so engrossed in their issues that we neglect our own well-being. This type of empathy can be harmful to both ourselves and the other person, as it can perpetuate unhealthy patterns and enable negative behavior.

One common scenario is when you find yourself alone, having reflected deeply on the repeated boundary violations, ultimately concluding that ending the relationship is necessary. You prepare yourself mentally for the challenging conversation, determined to firmly set your boundaries. However, as you confront the person, their tears and emotional outpouring evoke feelings of empathy within you, making it challenging to maintain your resolve.

You then adjust your behavior based on this one powerful feeling, disregarding all your previous thoughts, opinions, feelings, needs, limits, values, even temporarily forgetting about your hurt, your lack of emotional safety in that particular relationship, and your own unhappiness...just like that.

Toxic empathy doesn't allow you to feel your own feelings. When you experience toxic empathy, you lose your sense of self and your values are forgotten. What's worse, you could be inadvertently rewarding bad behavior without even realizing it. Toxic empathy prevents the situation that you are in from improving, and draws you back into the same cycles that have always existed over and over again.

Providing comfort and support to others is important, but it should not come at the cost of neglecting your own needs. People are responsible for their own actions, and enabling bad behavior by providing comfort without consequences is not beneficial in the long run. Consequences are important teachers of life.

Toxic Empathy and Covert Narcissists

It's all too easy to fall into the trap of toxic empathy when your genuine kindness and caring demeanor is manipulated and weaponized to keep you obedient and under another's control.

When dealing with a covert narcissist, one may get caught in toxic empathy in several ways:

- Feeling responsible for the narcissist's emotions: A covert narcissist will often make others feel guilty for their own emotions, and it's easy to get caught up in trying to make them feel better.

- Believing that the narcissist is a victim: Covert narcissists often play the role of a victim, making it easy for others to believe that they are in need of help and support. However, this can be a tactic to gain sympathy and attention, and to help them avoid doing the hard work of personal development and growth.

- Ignoring one's own needs: A covert narcissist may demand a lot of attention and emotional energy, leaving little room for others to take care of their own needs.

Toxic Empathy and Enablers

Toxic empathy can be a powerful force that prevents enablers in a narcissistic family system from seeing that they are the reason why the dysfunction continues.

Toxic empathy can deceive enablers into believing that they are helping by empathizing with the narcissist's perceived suffering and victimization, even at the expense of ignoring their self-destructive patterns. Enablers can become so attached to the narcissist's story that they become oblivious to the harm their enabling causes.

Enablers may also feel a strong sense of loyalty to the narcissist, especially if they are a close family member or spouse. They may feel that it is their duty to support and defend the narcissist, even if it means ignoring or minimizing the harm that is being inflicted on others and on themselves. This loyalty can be so strong that they become blind to the reality of the situation and the harm that is being caused.

Instead of addressing my mother's psychological issues, everyone enabled her. My father would sympathize with her, and his well-meaning behavior inadvertently reinforced her dysregulated behavior, even when it involved me. Year after year, he continued to deny that there was something wrong, opting instead to pacify her with sweets and ice cream to soothe her moods.

My father cautioned me against seeking professional help, insisting that "we will deal with it ourselves." Meanwhile, my older sibling chose to turn a blind eye to the situation, even laughing it off, dismissing my mother's behavior as normal and part of our cultural upbringing, despite the physical, psychological and emotional abuse that she would regularly put me through.

In my last year of contact with any of them, my father had a brief hospital stay, prompting my sibling to visit our mother and check if she needed assistance. It was during this visit that my sibling came to a striking realization about her complete incapacity to function in society. "It's crazy! She can't function normally at all," my sibling expressed, as if it was a shock to him.

Witnessing the denial of enablers catch up to them after years of perpetuating dysfunction was quite shocking for me, but this is what happens when the path of toxic empathy is chosen over the path of reason. Eventually, reality will catch up and as it does, the scapegoat must maintain their resolve to protect themselves. In my case. my mother's narcissism worsened as she aged. She continued to look for me as a means to release her anger even as an old woman. Her need to scapegoat me never stopped and her games continued for years, until I finally got the resolve to block everyone who enabled her.

I now have empathy for myself first and foremost, after a lifetime of having received none from my blood family.

Toxic Empathy and Relationships Beyond the Narcissistic Parent

Your empathy is like an open door, it welcomes others in, and allows them to connect with you on a deeper level. However, it's important to be cautious of who you allow to enter through that door, as those with self-serving intentions may use your empathy to manipulate and betray you.

Don't get me wrong, I am not suggesting for you to lock the door and throw away the key, but It's wise to put people through a personal screening process before you open your heart to them.

Friends who only reach out to you when they want something from you, are a prime example of how empathy can be exploited. They may use the "sandwich method" to deceive you into thinking they are genuinely checking in on you, when in reality, they haven't thought about you until they realized that you had something they wanted. Hell, they may not even genuinely like you, but keep a facade of friendship only to use you as a resource, and keep their options open.

They will suddenly show up or call, "out of the blue", initiate the conversation by feigning interest in you, inquiring about topics that they know are important to you, and displaying attentiveness to your replies. Following this, they will make a request, express a problem, or convey a need that they are aware you can meet. They will evoke your empathy by informing you that you are the only person who can satisfy their requirement and how immensely grateful they would be if you were to comply. The discussion will end with excessive praise for your willingness to assist. After fulfilling their request, that "friend" will remain out of touch for a significant period or until the next occasion they need your aid.

And when you are the one to reach out to them, you are met with excuses such as them being too busy with work, their projects and their lives to make time for you.

"They'll have to see if they can fit you into their busy schedule sometime..."

When we care about someone, we let them know that we do consistently, not only when we desire to be served. Your empathy does not help you in these situations. In fact, it is used against you.

The Benefit of Consequences

A consequence can be laid down regardless of you level of empathy or love for the other person. A consequence has nothing to do with the love that you hold for someone else, and everything to do with the love that you owe yourself. Loving someone else does not equate with there being less love left for you. This is a false limiting belief. Healthy love goes both ways and does not diminish anyone, rather it elevates everyone. It is important to shift your perception of consequences and understand the value they can bring to your relationships. Consequences can be a powerful tool in fostering healthy, respectful interactions with others. By setting clear boundaries and holding people accountable for their actions, you are able to communicate your expectations for how you want to be treated. Furthermore, by enforcing consequences, you are showing self-respect and setting a standard for how you will not tolerate being treated. In order to break the cycle of toxic relationships, you must learn to prioritize your own well-being and use consequences as a means of protecting yourself and promoting healthy interactions.

For example, if someone shares your personal information without permission, a consequence could be for you to no longer share personal information with that person. Another example could be if someone repeatedly shows up late, a consequence could be to set a specific time at which the person must arrive or the plans will be cancelled. This has absolutely nothing to do with your love for the other person, and everything to do with you respecting yourself, your time and your resources. You can show empathy for the other person, while also showing yourself the same level of empathy and self-respect. These two concepts can absolutely co-exist. When communicating consequences, a person is making it clear that they value and respect themselves. A consequence is not "I don't love you". Rather it is, "I love myself too. Let's work together to strengthen this relationship as two equals who respect each other."

The Purpose of Consequences

- To protect yourself from further harm.
- To promote change and prevent the individual from continuing their bad behaviors.
- To empower yourself and take control of the situation.
- To break the cycle of neglecting your own needs.
- To promote healthy relationships based on mutual respect and trust.
- To reduce feelings of guilt and shame.
- To reduce enabling behaviors and co-dependency.
- To foster your autonomy and take ownership of your life.
- To prioritize your own needs and engage in self-care.
- To promote accountability and personal development.

Without consequences, there is no learning, no

growth and no improvement. Toxic empathy only enables. It does not heal, help, or solve anything.

Wiggle Your Toes

If a wave of toxic empathy overwhelms you, ground yourself. Wiggle your toes and feel the weight of your body on your feet. Focus on that feeling for a moment and then remember:

In the physical space that you occupy, and on the two feet that you stand on, another person's wiggling of their toes, is not something that you can feel in your own shoes, is it? You can only feel the sensation of your toes inside your own shoes.

That's not to say that you couldn't have an excellent idea of what people are feeling when they wiggle their toes. You may imagine how they might be feeling, you may sympathize if they are hurting, or you may even coordinate the wiggling of your toes together and create a bond in such a way! But the fact still remains...

You can't feel their toes in your shoes. You don't know if their feet are cold or hot, sweaty or dry, if the skin is sensitive or rough. Are they wearing socks? Are those socks cotton? Polyester? What if they are wearing socks and you are not? What if they are wearing boots and you are wearing flip-flops? Would the feeling still be the same? You will never feel what they feel from the perspective of their own body. Your feelings are your own and come from your body.

Toxic empathy fools you into believing that the feeling of your own toes wiggling belongs to someone else.

Using Anger Healthily to Kill Toxic-Guilt and Toxic Empathy

It is perfectly valid for you to feel anger for having been robbed of your right to having a healthy, loving, and safe family.

Allowing yourself to feel and express anger is an important step towards healing. Anger is a natural and healthy emotion in response to being mistreated, and it can be a powerful motivator for change. By acknowledging and expressing your anger, you are acknowledging that you deserve better. You are acknowledging that mistreatment is not acceptable.

Furthermore, anger can help you establish healthy boundaries and assert your needs and wants. It be a catalyst for action. It can motivate you to watch your own behavior and ensure that you never become like your narcissistic parent, make changes in your life, and empower you to take control of your circumstances. It is important to note that expressing anger in a healthy way does not mean being aggressive or violent towards others. It means acknowledging and processing your emotions in a way that allows you to move forward positively and constructively.

Use your anger as a motivator for change. Recognize that you have the power to break free from the cycle of guilt and shame that the narcissistic family system has instilled in you. Use your anger to challenge the false beliefs that you've been taught, and to redefine your sense of self-worth and value.

Journal Prompts

- Write down all the ways in which toxic guilt manifests through you and then challenge each of those toxic thoughts.
- How can you use this experience of toxic guilt to set boundaries and protect yourself in future relationships?
- How can you learn from this experience and not repeat unhealthy patterns in the future?
- Write down the names of all the people who have enabled the narcissist and list all the ways in which they have let you down. Allow yourself to

express the anger that you may feel towards the people who enabled your dysfunctional narcissistic family system.
- What messages did you receive growing up about expressing anger? How can you reframe those messages to support healthy anger expression?

The Lessons Learned

Healing from the emotional burden of guilt and shame is a process that may take time to fully overcome. Learning to identify and recognize the signs of guilt manifesting within you will help you to separate yourself from it. It's important to remember that guilt is a feeling, not a part of your identity. When you become aware of the presence of guilt in your body, you can choose not to believe it and work on letting it go.

You have no control over how your family members choose to cope with such dysfunction and they may choose to ignore it, remain in denial, or even turn against you for speaking out about the traumas that they caused you.

In any case, all you can do is prioritize your own well-being and not let guilt manipulate you into conforming to the dysfunctional rules of a narcissistic family system.

Learn to detect guilt when it manifests in your body, and as you do, ask yourself some questions. Is this guilt healthy or unhealthy? Am I taking on someone else's responsibilities on my shoulders? Am I being held responsible for someone else's inability to control themselves? Am I feeling guilty for laying down boundaries as to how I want to be treated as a person? As you begin to practice asking yourself these important questions, you may notice that the burdens on your shoulders begin to diminish.

Trust your own actions and decisions. You did what you had to do to survive and protect yourself. The journey to healing may be difficult, but remember that you are still standing and it will get better. Keep pushing forward, trust the process and take care of yourself. Love and trust yourself.

Never Feel Guilty For:

- Ending a toxic relationship or any relationship that no longer serves you.
- People's misguided views, misplaced resentment, or false beliefs about you.
- Saying no when you need to set boundaries or prioritize your well-being.
- Making mistakes.
- Setting and enforcing healthy boundaries to protect yourself and your time.
- Speaking your truth and asserting your needs in a respectful way.
- Changing your mind.
- Taking your time to respond and honoring your own pace.
- Honoring your limits and not overextending yourself.
- Prioritizing your safety and well-being.
- Ghosting an unsafe person.
- Falling out of love.
- Asking for help when you need it.
- Getting sick or experiencing a relapse in your mental or physical health.
- Standing up for what you believe in.
- Pursuing your dreams and passions, even if they may not align with others' expectations.
- Finding your happiness and taking steps to prioritize your own joy and fulfillment.
- Living authentically and embracing your true self, regardless of societal or familial pressure.
- Making your own life choices while recognizing that other people's life choices are their own.

Chapter 12

Grief

It's Ok Not to Be OK: Grief

I was just a toddler, eagerly awaiting my father's return home. I would run to him and jump up and down, anticipating the moment he would pick me up. As soon as he did, a sense of relief washed over me—the comfort of resting my head on his shoulder, feeling protected and safe knowing that my dad was home. I can still vividly recall that feeling, that bond, as if it enfolded me in a bubble of safety. It was but an elusive and innocent glimpse into the past, of what a parent's love, that bond, once felt like for me.

I held onto the bond I felt towards my father all my life, despite the times my mother punished me as a child for refusing to participate in her damning stories about him when he wasn't home. My defiance only intensified her hatred towards me. She would always tell me that I am just like my father, with a smirk of contempt on her face, thinking that it would be taken as an insult. However, I was proud to be like my father, because to me he embodied strength and bravery—qualities that I aspired to possess myself.

But coming to the realization that the "good parent", the one I idealized, defended, and looked up to, was actually a bigger threat to my safety than my mother was, shattered my illusions and left me feeling empty. It was my love for him that kept me within her grasp. He was not a safe person for me. He was an enabler, a flying monkey, and at the end of the day, he served her. And so, I had to let that feeling go. As I grieved for the father who should have been there, who was out there somewhere, and who abandoned me, I faced the emptiness of the space I had reserved for him. I faced the emptiness of being the unloved daughter of a narcissistic mother. I faced many empty spaces for what should have been.

It was a strange experience to mourn only emptiness.

I also grieved for the empty space of the person I could have been—the dreams that disintegrated, the aspirations I always wanted to pursue but never did. I longed for a sense of belonging, for a big family with aunts, uncles, and cousins—something I never experienced due to the isolation imposed by my parents' life choices. I never got to know any extended family member, and perhaps it was better that way, considering how my mother would speak horribly of me during those phone calls abroad.

I had to allow myself the time and space to sink into the darkness for a while. It felt like it would last forever. But it didn't. As the grief began to subside, new dreams and aspirations revealed themselves to me.

I reflected inwardly, thinking, "The breath of life still flows through me. With the time I have left on Earth, there are countless things I can accomplish. My experiences can be a catalyst for positive change in others' lives. Someday, as my descendants trace our family tree, maybe they will recognize that I was the one who broke the cycle of generational trauma. And even if they don't, I will find solace in knowing that I did my part to pave the way for a better future.

Leaving a narcissistic family system can be a journey that feels like you're walking on a tightrope, balancing between the past and the future, and the grief you may feel is unique.

You may feel burdened by a heavy weight, a mix of confusion, despair, emptiness, guilt, anger, disbelief, and a deep sense of injustice. These emotions are valid and deserve acknowledgment. It's important to give yourself permission to feel and process them in your own time and in your own way.

Your grieving process is likely to involve confronting two distinct layers.

The first layer involves mourning the family you yearned for, the one you envisioned based on societal expectations or fleeting moments of connection. This could be the family you dreamt of having unconditional love from, the one you believed existed if you just tried harder, or the one you saw glimpses of in movies or books. Grieving this loss can involve feelings of longing, sadness, and anger. It's the anger of unmet needs, broken promises, and the frustration of a reality that never materialized.

The second layer involves confronting the reality of your family and letting go of the idealized version you clung to. This can be a painful process of acknowledging the abuse and manipulation you endured. You may grieve the loss of innocence, the hope that things would change, or the belief that there was once love. Disillusionment and a sense of betrayal are common emotions at this stage. As you process this layer, a gradual acceptance of the truth can begin to emerge.

Radical acceptance is painful, and yet it is the key to going forward.

It's important to understand that neither idealized version was your fault. The first stemmed from a natural human desire for love and belonging, while the second was a coping mechanism for surviving a dysfunctional environment.

Grieving is a natural process, and there's no right or wrong way to navigate it.

By giving ourselves permission to grieve, we effectively close the door on past pain and open a new door leading toward the light at the end of the tunnel. As we navigate through the grieving process, we gradually diminish the hold that pain and trauma have over us until they become mere chapters in our story. It's the story of a survivor—one marked by resilience, strength, and growth.

Carl Jung's quote encapsulates this journey perfectly: "The darker the shadow, the brighter the light."

Grief can be a transformative experience, as it helps you to understand your own feelings and needs more deeply. On the other side of grief, you'll find that the world looks different. The colors will be more vibrant, the sunshine will be warmer, and the birds will sing louder. You'll learn to appreciate the small things in life, like a hug, a warm cup of tea, or the feeling of the sun on your face. You'll learn that beyond the grief, there is a stronger and more resilient version of yourself, one who has shed the skin of the scapegoat and is ready to embrace a new chapter in life.

You'll find yourself, for the first time, as a whole person, and this is something worth holding on to.

The Scapegoat's Grieving Journey

Leaving a narcissistic family system involves a multitude of losses, each triggering a unique kind of grief.

- Shattered Relationships: The loss of connection with family members, including parents, siblings, and extended family. This can be particularly painful, as family is often seen as a source of unconditional love and support.

- Lost Identity and Belonging: The loss of a sense of belonging within the family unit. The scapegoat may have difficulty defining themselves without the negative label assigned by the family.

- Emotional Abandonment: The loss of emotional support and validation from family members.

This can leave the scapegoat feeling isolated, misunderstood, and questioning their own reality.

- Unmet Needs: The loss of financial or material support that a healthy family might provide.

- Tainted Memories: The loss of a healthy perspective on childhood memories. Happy times may be overshadowed by the constant tension and negativity.

- Erosion of Security: The loss of a sense of security and stability that a healthy family environment fosters.

- Shattered Illusions: The loss of the belief that the family truly loved them and had good intentions. This can be one of the most profound and painful aspects of grief.

- Loss of Normalcy: The loss of a sense of normalcy. Growing up in a narcissistic family can skew the scapegoat's perception of healthy family dynamics.

- Diminished Hope: The loss of hope for ever being seen, heard, or validated by the family. This can lead to feelings of hopelessness and despair.

- Isolation and Loneliness: The feeling of isolation and loneliness that often accompanies disconnecting from the family unit.

- Invalidated Trauma: The feeling of injustice for having their experiences and trauma denied or minimized by the family.

- Loss of Dreams: The scapegoat may grieve the opportunities or dreams they were forced to abandon due to the dysfunctional family environment.

- Loss of Self-Esteem: Years of abuse and negativity can take a toll on the scapegoat's self-esteem, leading to grief over the person they could have been.

- Loss of Potential: The grief may extend to the potential for healthy relationships and a fulfilling life that was hindered by the family dynamics.

The Stages of Grief

The Kubler-Ross model, outlining denial, anger, bargaining, depression, and acceptance, offers a framework for understanding this process. However, it's important to remember that grief is not linear, and the scapegoat may revisit stages or experience them simultaneously.

- Denial: In this stage, the scapegoat may minimize or even deny the abuse they endured. They might cling to the hope of a loving family, repressing painful memories (tainted memories) and clinging to idealized versions of the past.

- Anger: As denial crumbles, anger often takes center stage. The scapegoat may be furious at the narcissist and other family members who enabled the abuse. This anger can be coupled with guilt or shame, creating a confusing emotional cocktail.

- Bargaining: Desperate for connection or a change in the family dynamic, the scapegoat might engage in bargaining. They may try to appease the narcissist or change their behavior in a futile attempt to win approval or love.

- Depression: The weight of the losses, shattered relationships (lost sense of belonging), emotional abandonment, and invalidated experiences can lead to deep sadness and despair. The scapegoat may feel isolated, hopeless, and question their own reality.

- Acceptance: This doesn't mean condoning the abuse, but rather acknowledging the truth of the situation. The scapegoat may grieve the loss of dreams (loss of potential) alongside the anger of having their experiences invalidated. Acceptance allows them to detach emotionally and start building a healthy life outside the toxic family system.

Journal Prompts

- What was the "family narrative" you believed in for most of your life? How does it differ from the reality you're facing now?
- Is there a specific incident or realization that triggered a shift in your understanding of your family dynamics? Describe it.
- What is the biggest loss you're grieving right now (e.g., lost relationship with a parent, lost sense of belonging)?
- Is there anger you need to express towards specific family members? Write it down without judgment.
- What parts of yourself did you suppress due to the family dynamic?
- What does "letting go" mean to you in the context of your family?
- What are some positive affirmations you can repeat to yourself during times of self-doubt or sadness?
- Imagine your future self, healed and thriving. What message would they give to you right now?

A Word of Comfort

Grief is a chasm that carves out a hollow space in the soul, leaving an ache that feels like such an empty space shouldn't exist within us, and yet it does. As survivors, we mourn the loss of those we hold dear, grappling with the realization that the love we thought filled that space was a mirage all along. The absence of what we long for is palpable, and the love we believed was genuine turns out to be nothing but a cruel illusion.

Yet, amidst the darkness, there is a glimmer of hope. A light that shines at the end of the tunnel, beckoning us forward. It may be difficult to discern at first, but it's there, waiting for us to find it. Our minds may be consumed by the trauma and the grief, unable to see the path ahead. But with time, healing and clarity will come, revealing a way forward from the depths of our sorrow.

Healing is not a linear process and you will have your good days and bad days.

On good days, you may feel more in control of your emotions, more hopeful about the future and more able to cope with the aftermath of the narcissistic family system. You may feel like you are making progress and that healing is possible. On bad days, you may feel overwhelmed by the intensity of your emotions, feel like you're not making any progress, or that you're stuck in the same place. You may feel like the pain and trauma are too much to bear. These bad days are a normal part of the healing process.

Self-care, self-compassion, and self-love are essential for nourishing your soul during the journey of healing from grief. In time, you will learn to fill that empty space within you with true love. Until then, do things that make you feel good and that bring you a sense of peace. Be kind and understanding towards yourself, recognize that you are going through a difficult time and acknowledge that it's okay to not be okay. Be gentle with yourself and be patient, healing takes time.

As you walk across this bridge, know that on the other side, awaits a healthier, and peaceful future.

Chapter 13

The Things Beyond Your Control

Letting the Cards Fall Where They May: Radical Acceptance

When I made the choice to go no contact, I grappled with the harsh reality that their distorted perceptions of me would persist far beyond anyone who knew them or had ties to them, branding me as the villain who selfishly abandoned their family for mysterious and selfish reasons.

I was acutely aware that my mother's fabricated stories would continue to garner sympathy from others, painting me as the villain in her tales of victimhood. Equally frustrating was the golden child's persistent refusal to acknowledge the lifelong impact of my mother's actions on my well-being. Additionally, my father's twisted vision of love would undoubtedly persist, as though my struggles were nothing more than exaggerated inconveniences to be brushed aside in the "bigger picture". Initially, facing these harsh truths felt like an insurmountable defeat, and accepting that

I couldn't change this false narrative, one that they all decided to perpetuate, weighed heavily on my heart.

However, with time, I came to realize that prioritizing my own well-being, my self-preservation, and my peace over my need for validation and acceptance from those who had caused me so much pain was, in reality, a victory.

This was me, reclaiming ownership of my life, without seeking or needing anyone's permission or approval. It was an empowering thought.

Removing ourselves from environments that cause us harm entails acknowledging that these environments will persist unchanged. This acceptance of reality is a crucial step toward healing and growth for the scapegoat.

It's widely acknowledged that the dynamics of a narcissistic family system often persist even after the scapegoat—the apparent problem—leaves. This enduring pattern stems from the fact that the scapegoat was never the cause of the family issues in the first place but rather a product of the dysfunctional narcissistic family dynamic.

The reality is that the dysfunction will continue, with conversations left unspoken and realities denied as everyone continues to tiptoe around the narcissist, just as they always did, to avoid becoming the next target. The primary focus remains, as it always did, on appeasing the narcissist to maintain a fragile peace, rather than addressing the dysfunction directly.

Inevitably, a new scapegoat may be designated, perpetuating the cycle while others dance around the issues to avoid conflict, as they've always done.

True change must originate from within the family dynamics themselves, in other words, from meaningful change in the family's culture. However, when members are unwilling to confront reality and address the underlying issues, effecting transformation becomes a near-impossible task. In such instances, it's imperative to recognize that the situation is beyond your control, prompting a shift in focus towards self-preservation and personal development.

Taking the necessary time to reflect and process your feelings before letting go and moving forward is necessary for healing. Reflecting on past experiences, lessons learned, personal growth, and the genuine desire for release can facilitate the process of radical acceptance.

Acknowledging what cannot be changed and prioritizing your well-being must become your central focus. Though cutting ties may feel like severing a part of yourself, holding onto pain only perpetuates suffering. As you take the time needed to process and let go, the hard work of embracing change and preparing to emerge on the other side becomes the next step towards better being.

What's Holding You Back?

Despite the earnest desire to embrace radical acceptance, the path for a scapegoat is inevitably riddled with challenges. A lingering hope that the family will one day acknowledge our suffering and offer an apology can hold us back, keeping us tethered to the past and waiting for validation that may never come. Years of enduring gaslighting and manipulation can leave us questioning our own memories and perceptions, making it difficult to accept a clear narrative of our experience. Fear of isolation, particularly if we lack support systems outside the family, makes the process even more daunting.

Recognizing the ways in which we fall into these circular patterns is a significant first step toward breaking those loops. Although breaking free from these thought patterns can be challenging, redirecting our focus back to ourselves, nurturing self-trust and self-compassion, becomes a vital component of the healing process. While it may seem like scaling a mountain, self-awareness is an indispensable aspect of the journey toward healing.

Having said this, here are the toxic loops that you must become aware of, which may keep you trapped and unable to move forward:

- Future Thinking: Clinging to the belief that the family will someday change or apologize can keep the scapegoat tethered to the past, waiting for validation that may never come.

- Past Thinking: Yearning for a loving family unit that never truly existed can make the reality of the situation even harder to accept.

- Fear of the Unknown: Severing ties with family can mean losing the only known support system, even if it's dysfunctional. Building new connections can feel daunting.

- Fear of Rejection: The scapegoat may desperately crave the love and approval withheld by the family, making letting go feel like giving up on ever being loved again.

- Low Self-Esteem: Years of abuse can leave the scapegoat with low self-esteem, making them question whether they deserve a healthy and supportive environment.

- Denial: Because of the psychological manipulation created by the entire family unit, the scapegoat may downplay the abuse they endured, creating a distorted reality that makes letting go seem unreasonable.

- Lack of Closure: The lack of a genuine apology or explanation from the family can leave the scapegoat feeling unresolved and stuck in the past.

- Guilt or Shame: The scapegoat may carry the burden of blame instilled by the family, making them feel responsible for the dysfunctional dynamic.

- Need for Control: Letting go can feel like relinquishing control over the narrative of the abuse. The scapegoat may fear the family will rewrite history and the impact that this will cause to them and their future may be a huge challenge to navigate.

- Emotional Attachment: Even after the abuse, there may still be a flicker of hope for a future reconciliation, making letting go emotionally difficult.

Take a moment to become mindful of the reasons why you may have difficulty letting go. Don't try to fix them as they come up, just accept them as they surface.

You feel how you feel and taking the time to validate yourself is an important step in crossing over to the other side.

Be sure to practice mindfulness so that you may detect and catch the negative pulls that hold you back as they manifest. When you become aware of the monsters within, you can gain control over them.

Empowered by Letting Go: Relinquishing Control

The thought loops that keep us trapped often lead to one inevitable realization: a distorted relationship with what we think we can control. As the family scapegoat, you have likely been conditioned to bear false burdens of responsibility that were never yours to carry in the first place. Blamed for others' emotions, moods, decisions, and choices, you may have been conditioned to feel that everything that transpired with the narcissistic parent was within your control. However, this is a falsehood.

Understanding what you can control healthily and realistically, enables you to focus your energy and efforts on aspects of your life where you can effect positive change, fostering a sense of agency and autonomy. Conversely, recognizing what is beyond your control helps you let go of futile attempts to change situations or people who are unwilling or unable to change. This distinction empowers you to prioritize your well-being, set boundaries, and cultivate resilience in the face of challenges that cannot be altered.

The Things You Can't Control

- Their Perceptions: You cannot control the distorted views or narratives the narcissist holds about you. Remember that these are projections, and attempting to change their minds requires introspection and self-awareness, which is beyond your influence.

- The Past: The pain and experiences you endured cannot be altered. However, you can choose how you respond and make empowering decisions that prioritize your well-being and future growth.

- Their Actions: You have no control over how your family chooses to react to your boundaries or expression of authenticity. They may attempt manipulation, guilt-tripping, or sabotage, but their behavior is not within your control.

- External Events: Life is unpredictable, and external events such as job losses, illnesses, or unexpected challenges are beyond your control.

- Their Future Choices: While your family may continue dysfunctional patterns, you cannot dictate their behavior. Their choices are theirs alone.

- Validation From Them: You cannot control whether they choose to validate you or not. Instead, focus on self-acceptance, self-respect, and cultivating your own sense of inner strength and worth.

- Outcomes Beyond Your Actions: You can control your boundaries and actions, but not the outcome of every situation. Be prepared for potential negative pushback when asserting healthy limits for yourself.

- Their Happiness: You cannot control your family's happiness, nor is it your responsibility. Focus on nurturing your own well-being instead.

- Ultimate Control: Understand that you do not have complete control over life itself. Embrace the power you do have in making choices that empower you and contribute to a life you value.

The Things In Your Control

- Steering Your Focus: You choose where your thoughts wander. Will you dwell on the past, or focus on building a brighter future? The direction you choose is yours.

- Charting Your Course: No longer bound by their expectations, you now get to decide how you'll live your life. Where do you want to go next? You are free to decide.

- Raising Your Sails: Let your drive and focus be the wind that propels you forward. Embrace resilience, curiosity, and harness your determination to face challenges head-on, knowing that prioritizing yourself leads to a brighter future.

- Setting Your Destination: Dream big! Set goals and aspirations that excite you. This is your roadmap to a fulfilling future.

- Tending Your Vessel: Self-care becomes your lifeline. Prioritize healthy habits that nourish your body, mind, and spirit. Invest in activities that bring you joy and peace.

- Communication: You get to choose how you communicate your needs and boundaries. Learn to express yourself assertively and prioritize open and honest relationships.

- Building Your Harbor: Surround yourself with supportive people who value you for who you are. Choose relationships that uplift and empower you.

- Shaping Your Surroundings: Create a safe space that reflects your values and fosters your wellbeing. You have the power to curate an environment that supports your growth and happiness.

Taking Back Control By Knowing Yourself

Discovering my values has been one of the most empowering tools on my healing journey. They serve as a guiding compass, illuminating the path towards making decisions that align with our true selves.

Growing up in a narcissistic family system has a lasting impact on our ability to trust ourselves and our judgments. Such families can condition us to prioritize external validation over our own instincts and self-reliance. In a sense, we have been trained to view self-differentiation as negative, as the narcissistic parent may have demonized any attempt at asserting our own identity and values.

However, identifying and understanding our core values can be a powerful tool in breaking this cycle and regaining our sense of control.

When we prioritize our values and make decisions based on them, we eliminate doubt and the need for validation from others. Instead of seeking confirmation from the outside world, we begin to evaluate the values of those around us, considering whether or not we want to allow them into our lives based on how closely their values align with ours.

This shift in perspective can be liberating. By living true to our values, we become whole and comfortable in our own skin. We no longer feel the need to conform to societal pressures or seek the approval of others. We can embrace solitude and the freedom that comes with it, knowing that we are living a life that is true to ourselves.

Finding Your Values

Our values represent what truly matters to us at any given moment, guiding our decisions and actions toward the life we envision. However, our values aren't rigid; they shift and evolve as we grow, learn, and experience life's ups and downs. Major events, like starting a family or changing careers, can reshape our values, reflecting our changing priorities and perspectives. This is a natural part of life.

One common challenge arises when we profess certain values but struggle to live by them consistently. For example, we might say we value kindness, yet find ourselves being judgmental or impatient in certain situations. Becoming aware of these inconsistencies is key to living a more authentic life.

By consciously recognizing and honoring our values, we empower ourselves to make choices that align with our true selves. This awareness helps us stay true to what matters most, even when faced with difficult decisions or external pressures.

When we live in alignment with our values, we gain a sense of control over our lives.

Questions to Help Identify Your Core Values

- What are the things that bring me the most joy and fulfillment in my life?

- What am I the most proud of?
- What are the things that I am willing to stand up for, even if it means facing opposition or criticism from others?
- What are the principles that guide my decisions and actions?
- What are the qualities that I admire most in others, and strive to embody in myself?
- What are the causes or issues that I am most passionate about, and feel compelled to support or advocate for?
- What are the things that I am willing to make sacrifices for, because they are so important to me?
- What are the things that I am not willing to compromise on, even if it means missing out on other opportunities?
- What are the things that I am most proud of in my life, and why are they important to me?
- What are the things that I would like to be remembered for, and what does that say about my core values?
- What are the things that I fear the most losing, and why are they so valuable to me?

Take a look at the following list of values and choose the top ten that resonate with you the most.

Accountability	Altruism	Ambition
Authenticity	Balance	Beauty
Boldness	Candor	Care
Charity	Cleanliness	Collaboration
Commitment	Compassion	Competence
Confidence	Connection	Consciousness
Consistency	Cooperation	Courage
Courtesy	Creativity	Curiosity
Decency	Dependability	Determination
Discipline	Diversity	Empathy
Excellence	Fairness	Faith
Family	Flexibility	Focus
Forgiveness	Freedom	Friendship
Generosity	Gentleness	Gratitude
Growth	Happiness	Harmony
Health	Honesty	Honor
Hope	Humility	Imagination
Innovation	Integrity	Intelligence
Intensity	Joy	Justice
Kindness	Knowledge	Leadership
Learning	Liberty	Love
Loyalty	Mindfulness	Moderation
Modesty	Open-mindedness	Optimism
Orderliness	Patience	Peace
Perseverance	Playfulness	Practicality
Prudence	Punctuality	Purposefulness
Reliability	Respect	Responsibility
Self-discipline	Selflessness	Sensitivity
Service	Simplicity	Sincerity
Steadfastness	Strength	Support
Tactfulness	Thankfulness	Tolerance
Trust	Understanding	Unity
Vision	Wisdom	Wonder
Zeal		

Journal Prompts

- How do your values differ from your family's narrative?
- What part of yourself do you feel like you're losing by distancing yourself from the family?
- Imagine your future self, fully living aligned with your core values, healed, and thriving. What advice

would they give to you right now?
- Make a list of the things you once believed were in your control, but in fact, were not.

The Lessons Learned

Imagine a seed struggling for life in a barren environment. By letting the wind carry it away from the harsh landscape and to fertile ground, it can finally blossom into its full potential. This is akin to the journey a scapegoat undertakes after breaking free from a narcissistic family.

Radical acceptance empowers you to shed false hope and rewrite your narrative. Through this process, you will come to realize that your worth is intrinsic, not dictated by the labels or expectations of others. This newfound self-belief paves the way for setting healthy boundaries and prioritizing your own well-being.

The road ahead may hold uncertainties, but remember, every step you take toward self-discovery and healing is a victory. Embrace the courage to follow your heart, for within your response to life's challenges lies immense power.

Chapter 14

Meet Your Shadow

Becoming Aware of Our Programming

Have you ever had the experience of waking up one morning and having a song stuck in your head? And maybe you actually liked that song, so when you were on your way to work, you turned it on and blasted it in your car. It is always lovely to listen to a feel-good tune, isn't it? And as you do, you may enjoy the feeling that this song brings back, such as the good old party days, or maybe that time when you went to see a band live in concert for the first time. This feeling that this song elicited within you put you in a great mood.

Or maybe you had the opposite reaction because the song that you woke up to was "Row, row, row your boat," and that was such an annoying song to have in your head at eight in the morning! As you drove yourself to work, you made sure to blast other songs in the car so you could get that song out of your head.

But whether you liked or hated that song, doesn't change the fact that it has been stored in your mind, and for whatever reason, it jumped out of its storage drawer and was brought to your conscious attention on that particular morning. Did you put that song in there by yourself, or was it in there because you heard it repeatedly throughout the course of your life?

Why did it just suddenly pop into your head? Did

something trigger it? Did you have a dream? Or maybe it popped up for no reason at all? Funny how the mind can sometimes bring buried things to the surface, without us consciously doing anything to try and recollect that memory in the first place.

Everything that you have ever experienced is still alive and well in the depths of your subconscious mind.

What if I say: "Row, row, row your boat gently down the..."

Did you finish that sentence automatically in your head? Did you automatically say stream?

And your belief that the ending of that sentence being stream is pretty much set in stone isn't it? It's not something that you would question because you have heard it so often during your upbringing. Everybody that ever sang that song ended that sentence with stream. And so now, your automatic reaction may be to say stream without questioning yourself.

Did you think stream automatically without questioning yourself?

But what if some of the beliefs that you do not question and that lie stored deeply in your mind are the things that your narcissistic parent repeated to you over and over during your upbringing? Like: "No one could ever love someone like you?" or "There is something wrong with you." And what if that repetition was inadvertently internalized, just like the boat song was? And what if "No one could ever love you" drives your automatic responses, in the exact same way that you automatically responded, "stream" when you saw "Row, row, row, your boat, gently down the...."?

It doesn't matter if you like the song or not. Ultimately, the way you will sing it is shaped by the lyrics that you internalized.

Understanding the origins of your thoughts is important for recognizing their impact on your psyche. By acknowledging that some of your beliefs were learned rather than being ultimate truths, you can begin to challenge and reframe them.

The Shadow Self

In Jungian philosophy, the concept of the shadow self pertains to those aspects of our personality that we struggle to accept, leading us to unconsciously attempt to ignore, repress, or outright deny them. It's a universal tendency for people to perceive themselves as inherently good, to justify their actions, and to believe in the accuracy of their thought patterns. Consequently, acknowledging our darker tendencies can be challenging, prompting us to rationalize our negative behaviors with explanations and narratives. This avoidance of our shadow self represents a formidable psychological hurdle to overcome.

No one is perfect, and part of us knows this to be true. While it's easy to notice other people's imperfections, it's not always easy to acknowledge our own. We're often reluctant to admit our own flaws, and many of us develop defense mechanisms to avoid confronting our shadow selves.

Admitting to ourselves when we're feeling jealous or judgmental, or when we're angry and fail to take responsibility for our actions, can be challenging. Similarly, accepting different points of view can be difficult, as we all like to think of ourselves as open-minded until we're faced with a challenging situation.

It can be challenging to acknowledge that we struggle to process our emotions in a healthy way, leading us to avoid addressing these emotions when they arise in our loved ones. Reflecting on our past decisions and taking responsibility for their painful outcomes, particularly in dire circumstances, is also daunting.

Even accepting constructive criticism can feel extremely painful and triggering, as we've already been criticized throughout our lifetime. We never want to hear another reminder that brings us back to the criticism the narcissist incessantly forced us to endure day after day. Thus, we often find ourselves triggered, responding with various defense mechanisms to shield ourselves from any reminder of their toxic words, regardless of the context.

Another daunting realization we may encounter during the process of shadow work is that we've internalized some of our abusers' character traits—a deeply unsettling notion to confront. Unfortunately, growing up with dysfunctional caretakers increases the likelihood of adopting certain traits from them; it's an inevitable aspect of human nature.

Balancing the task of silencing our inner-critic, silencing our ego, and looking squarely at ourselves is no easy thing to do.

The narcissists were adept at finding weaknesses and flaws, and weaponizing them to justify their victimhood and excuse their abusive behavior. As a result, we may never have developed a healthy relationship with ourselves as a whole, instead unconsciously operating under a feeling, a certain haze, dictating that we need to be perfect to love ourselves, and yet are never good enough. We may find ourselves constantly adjusting our own standards for self-acceptance.

And so, the purpose of shadow work becomes significant, as it enables us to confront the deepest and scariest parts of ourselves so that we may then learn to work with it, ultimately freeing ourselves from its control. Regardless of what arises within you, it's important to recognize that we all embody both light and shadows. Your shadows alone do not define you, nor does the light. As Carl Jung aptly stated, "One does not become enlightened by imagining figures of light, but by making the darkness conscious."

You are not defined by your upbringing; you are uniquely you, with the agency to choose how to navigate the lessons imparted to you. As we gain awareness of our shadow, it will no longer have the power to control the direction of our lives.

This brings me to the flip side of all this: our shadow isn't just a Mariana Trench filled with darkness. It is also a deep unexplored ocean of untapped potential, talent, and gifts. Tapping into this potential is very rewarding, but it comes as a package deal; it's the yin and the yang of life, one cannot exist without the other. We must deal with our entirety to access our untapped potential.

The practice of integrating our subconscious mind into our active conscious mind is necessary to unlock the mysteries of who we are, as whole and balanced people. By learning to accept ourselves as we are and integrate all aspects of our personality into our daily lives, we may find that life becomes much easier, more fulfilling, and joyful.

A support system is always recommended when one takes on the monumental task of stripping away the falsehoods that we tell ourselves, and when we decide to finally face the creatures that reside in our hearts. Be mindful of undertaking shadow work alone. It is better to have someone to talk to, and who can help keep you grounded in the process. You may find that the rabbit hole goes very deep, and at times, it can get very daunting.

The Path of Shadow Work

The path of shadow work marks the initiation into a profound journey of self-discovery and transformation. It begins with a courageous step into the depths of our psyche, where our shadow selves reside, harboring the aspects of our personality that we have repressed, denied, or deemed unacceptable.

The first stage of beginning shadow work involves cultivating self-awareness. This means turning inward with honesty and openness, observing our thoughts, emotions, and behaviors without judgment. Through practices such as meditation, journaling, or introspection, we start to unravel the layers of our unconscious mind, shining a light on the hidden corners of our psyche.

As we delve deeper into self-awareness, we begin to identify the patterns and triggers that signal the presence of our shadow. These may manifest as recurring conflicts in relationships, self-sabotaging behaviors, or persistent feelings of fear, anger, or shame. Recognizing these patterns is crucial as they serve as signposts guiding us towards the aspects of ourselves that require healing and integration.

With awareness comes the willingness to confront our shadow selves. This requires courage and vulnerability as we face the parts of ourselves that we have long avoided or suppressed. It may involve revisiting past traumas, acknowledging our deepest fears, or confronting the aspects of ourselves that we find uncomfortable or shameful.

Throughout this process, self-compassion is paramount. We must extend kindness and understanding to ourselves as we navigate the complexities of our inner world. It's natural to encounter resistance or discomfort when confronting our shadow, but by embracing these challenges with patience and empathy, we create space for healing and growth to unfold.

Triggers

When you allow yourself to be honest with yourself, you are also able to be honest with others - Carl Jung.

Knowing our triggers doesn't only point to our wounds; they also illuminate our shadow self – the parts of ourselves that we have ignored, pushed away, and may harbor feelings of hatred toward.

Carl Jung proposed that when we struggle to accept our own painful emotions, we subconsciously try to avoid them in others. This can lead us to activate defense mechanisms towards the wrong people or situations. Blinded by the intensity of these triggered emotions, we misinterpret the present moment and reality.

This may in turn point to personality traits that we may not want to admit to ourselves as having, such as defensiveness, hostility, or emotional volatility. Acknowledging and accepting these aspects of ourselves can be challenging, but it remains nonetheless necessary for our growth and healing.

The key to overcoming triggers lies in self-awareness. Through mindfulness, we can learn to identify our triggers and the limiting beliefs they activate. This self-knowledge empowers us to respond more consciously, preventing triggers from controlling our behavior.

Projections

When we survive a dysfunctional family and are raised by a narcissist, it's often evident when their behavior is a projection onto us. However, what about our own projections onto others? This is a phenomenon that can happen to anyone, and becoming aware of our own projections is also an important step in doing our shadow work. We may have been taught to view the world through a lens of mistrust, where we are quick to jump to the conclusion that people we meet intentionally hurt us. While it's important to distinguish safe from unsafe, there is also the danger that because of our upbringing, we may project our shadow—everything that we have been taught to reject about ourselves—onto others.

Carl Jung taught us that projecting our undesirable feelings such as pent-up anger, stress, and unhappiness onto others is a common defense mechanism. For example, a boss who is feeling immense pressure to meet deadlines might constantly criticize an employee for minor mistakes. The criticism may seem justified on the surface, but the underlying reason could be the boss's own anxieties about performance, not the employee's actual work quality. By projecting their stress, the boss avoids dealing with it directly and creates a tense work environment for everyone.

A parent who never received enough praise from their own parents might constantly criticize their child's achievements. While the parent might believe they're pushing their child to excel, the criticism could be rooted in the parent's own unresolved feelings of inadequacy.

Someone scrolling through social media, bombarded with images of seemingly perfect lives, might lash out with negativity towards a friend's positive post. Their harsh comment might disguise their own feelings of insecurity or lack of fulfillment.

The real problem always arises when people justify their behaviors based on a feeling, yet never delve deeper within themselves to try and understand the true root cause of that feeling.

We Dislike in Others What We Can't Accept About Ourselves

When we meet a person, the general rule of thumb is that the character traits we notice about them and that we like or dislike, are a reflection of ourselves. This idea can be quite difficult to digest at first. When I discovered this concept, I thought of the people that revolted me, and the very thought that I would be just like them was even more revolting. But holding ourselves accountable for our judgments of others will help free us of the hatred that we feel towards ourselves.

For example, a person who constantly seeks the spotlight at social gatherings might rub you the wrong way. However, it could be that you crave attention in more subtle ways or have a hidden desire for validation. Their behavior might trigger a sense of competition for recognition.

Another example would be of a highly organized person who thrives on routine and dislikes clutter. They might find an artist's messy studio and spontaneous lifestyle utterly frustrating.

However, the organized person might discover a repressed desire for creativity and self-expression that their rigid schedule suppresses. They might be surprised to find a part of themselves that admires the artist's freedom and ability to live in the moment.

Patterns

Following instincts isn't good for you if you come from a dysfunctional family because your subconscious will lead you to unresolved feelings and you will re-experience your traumas over and over. Carl Jung said, "Our shadow self wants to be seen and accepted as a part of us."

If a mother has repeatedly told her child that they could never be loved, then the shadow side will say, "Let me show you how unlovable I can be." The shadow side doesn't know right from wrong, nor can it distinguish a joke from a serious statement. Whatever that parent repeats will be what the child will manifest unconsciously through their actions. The child will grow up repeating self-destructive patterns well into adulthood because the message imprinted deep in their subconscious by their own mother was that they are terrible and therefore don't deserve anything that is good for them. In fact, anything good that comes their way may trigger feelings of distrust, disdain, and even disgust. The body manifests what exists within the subconscious.

We may find that when we exit an abusive environment, we sometimes can't handle having too much of a good thing in our lives. I know that personally, I have sabotaged very good jobs, and have left places where I was made to feel welcome, all because there was a deep elusive feeling deep down inside that told me that I didn't belong there. A feeling that told me that I didn't belong and I needed to work harder and look further for happiness. I wasn't aware of what this feeling really was, as I was used to it and it was simply a part of how I felt daily. This was a feeling that I didn't question as I didn't even understand that I could look within for answers. But nonetheless, it drove all my decisions toward self-sabotaging behaviors. I never kept a good thing for very long. I always moved, moved, and moved, always looking for more and yet never feeling fulfilled no matter what came my way.

You might notice that when you try to change the course of your life for the better, you will feel a backward pull. For example, if you decide to go back to school, you might feel a rush of fear as you send in the application, almost making you regret having made a move. Or maybe if you have the opportunity for a healthy relationship, you may experience a sudden feeling to want to avoid that person. If you decide to launch a business, everything in your body will tell you to give up as soon as you hit that first obstacle. If you have a good job, no matter how well they treat you, you might keep feeling like there is always something better waiting for you elsewhere, or that you are a fraud.

Steps to Integrate the Shadow Side Into Your Conscious Personality:

1. Mindfulness: Pay attention to your thoughts, emotions, and physical sensations without judgment. This heightened awareness can reveal aspects you weren't consciously aware of.

2. Journaling: Free-write about your dreams, fears, recurring thoughts, and emotional triggers. This journaling practice can unearth hidden aspects of yourself and provide valuable clues about your shadow.

3. Emotional Reactions: Notice situations or people that evoke strong negative emotions like anger, sadness, or frustration. These emotional responses could be tied to your shadow.

4. Digging Deeper: When triggered, ask yourself: "What is this reminding me of?" This introspective question can unearth past experiences or beliefs associated with the trigger and the shadow emotions it activates.

5. Explore Your Shadow: Make a list of traits you dislike or judge in others. This could be arrogance, laziness, or neediness. These might be projections of your own shadow aspects you haven't fully accepted.

6. Art Therapy: Consider creative outlets like painting, drawing, or sculpting. Bypassing the limitations of

logic, these methods can bring unconscious shadow material to the surface for exploration.

7. Active Imagination: Developed by Carl Jung, this technique involves engaging in a dialogue with a personified aspect of your shadow. Imagine this shadow part as a character and have a conversation with it. This can shed light on its motivations and purpose.

8. Embrace and Integrate: Challenge negative labels you might associate with your shadow aspects. Are they truly who you are, or are they limiting beliefs you can shed?

9. Positive Aspects: Look for the positive potential within each shadow trait. For instance, anger can signal a need for healthy boundaries, and laziness can indicate a need for rest to fuel creativity.

10. Integration: Instead of suppressing your shadow, integrate it into your whole self. This doesn't mean indulging negative aspects, but acknowledging them and finding healthy ways to express their underlying energy.

Remember, integrating the shadow is not about eliminating negative aspects of yourself, but rather acknowledging and accepting them as part of who you are. By integrating the shadow, you can become a more authentic and whole person.

Journal Prompts

- Write down the name of a person in your life who you find difficult to be around (outside of the narcissistic family system) and list the specific negative traits or actions that bother you about them. Reflect on whether you possess any of these same traits or have engaged in similar actions in your own life.
- Think about the ways in which you have been holding yourself back from fully expressing yourself. What steps can you take to break free from these limitations and embrace your true self?
- Analyze your recurring dreams. What symbols or themes appear consistently? How might they connect to your shadow?

- Jung developed this technique where you engage in a dialogue with a personified aspect of your shadow. Imagine this shadow part as a character and have a conversation with it. What does it want you to know?
- The persona is the mask we wear in social situations. How does your persona differ from your authentic self? What shadow aspects might be hidden beneath the persona?

The Lessons Learned

The core lesson of shadow work emphasizes the importance of accepting all aspects of ourselves, both the "good" and the "bad."

When we embrace our shadow—that is, when we acknowledge and integrate those parts of ourselves that we may have deemed unacceptable or undesirable—we unlock a profound sense of authenticity. By accepting and owning our flaws, fears, and vulnerabilities, we cultivate a deeper understanding of ourselves and our experiences.

Furthermore, embracing our shadow enables us to develop emotional resilience. Rather than suppressing or denying uncomfortable emotions, we learn to navigate them with compassion and curiosity. This newfound resilience empowers us to face life's challenges with greater courage and grace.

Moreover, embracing our shadow paves the way for more meaningful and authentic relationships. When we accept ourselves fully, we are better equipped to connect with others on a genuine level. By embracing our own imperfections, we become more empathetic and accepting of the imperfections in others, fostering deeper connections and mutual understanding.

In essence, shadow work offers a pathway to wholeness by encouraging us to embrace the entirety of our being. Through this process, we discover that true authenticity and fulfillment arise not from perfection, but from the courageous acceptance of our complete selves.

"Until you make the unconscious conscious, it will direct your life and you will call it fate."
Carl Jung

Chapter 15

Challenging Limiting Beliefs

As you challenge yourself and slowly work towards self-acceptance and peace, you'll develop a unique perspective – your own brand of thought leadership. This isn't about arrogance or selfishness; it's about recognizing that you are not who the narcissistic parent painted you to be. It's about rewriting your own narrative and reframing how you see yourself.

Your mind has the power to take you as far as you allow it to, in any direction you choose. If you entertain thoughts that reinforce your lack of self-esteem, your daily actions and decisions will reflect that.

However, by acknowledging negative thoughts and consciously breaking the cycle, you can significantly improve your quality of life. When you find yourself at rock bottom, the only way to go is up. It's futile to indulge in self-defeating thoughts. Instead, challenge those thoughts and teach yourself to move in the opposite direction.

Always ask yourself: Is this thought beneficial for my well-being? If the answer is no, recognize that you may be grappling with a limiting belief that impedes your personal growth.

Limiting Beliefs

A limiting belief is a false and negative thought or assumption that you hold about yourself, which hinders you from realizing your full potential and achieving your goals. These beliefs can be deeply ingrained and obstruct you from living the life you desire. For survivors of a narcissistic family system, limiting beliefs can be particularly pervasive, as they have been repeatedly exposed to negative and invalidating messages about their worth and capabilities. Internalizing these messages can lead to the adoption of limiting beliefs that are difficult to identify and overcome.

Often, limiting beliefs operate beneath the surface, exerting influence over our actions and decisions without our conscious awareness. They manifest as an invisible force in your gut, sapping your energy, steering you toward choices that undermine your progress, and ultimately leaving you feeling defeated. Unconscious and deeply ingrained, these beliefs can be challenging to detect, acknowledge, and address.

However, it is possible to change limiting beliefs, but doing so requires diligent effort to become aware of the subconscious thoughts and beliefs that shape our behavior. Our subconscious mind significantly influences our daily actions and decisions, often guiding us on autopilot. By bringing these hidden beliefs to light, we can align our actions and decisions with our goals, paving the way for personal growth.

The Scapegoat's Common Limiting Beliefs

- Perceived As a Problem: The scapegoat may have internalized the constant criticism directed towards them, leading them to believe that they were inherently flawed or responsible for family issues. This could have contributed to feelings of worthlessness and a belief that they were inherently "bad."

- The Isolation of the Scapegoat: The narcissist may have actively isolated the scapegoat from supportive relationships, fostering a sense of loneliness and reinforcing the belief that they were unlovable.

- Basic Needs as Privileges: The scapegoat may have been conditioned to prioritize the emotional needs of others over their own well-being. This could have created a sense that their needs were unimportant and fostered resentment.

- Perceived Weakness: The scapegoat may have internalized the belittlement of their abilities and goals, leading them to feel inadequate and believing that they were incapable of success.

- The Burden of Unfounded Blame: The scapegoat may have shouldered blame for situations beyond their control, leading to feelings of guilt and confusion.

- The Perception of Inadequacy: The scapegoat may have constantly compared themselves to others and found lacking, resulting in a deep-seated belief that they were fundamentally flawed.

Limiting Beliefs and Cognitive Distortions

Cognitive distortions are patterns of thinking that are inaccurate or irrational. These thought patterns can reinforce limiting beliefs and make them more difficult to overcome. Cognitive distortions can be subtle, and we may not even be aware that we are engaging in them.

Our limiting beliefs often create the perfect environment for cognitive distortions to thrive. When we believe that we are not good enough or that we can't do anything right, we are more likely to engage in negative thought patterns that reinforce those beliefs. For example, if we believe that we are not good enough, we may engage in magnification, where we magnify our mistakes and minimize our successes, leading us to believe that we are indeed not good enough.

Limiting beliefs are the beliefs we hold about ourselves and the world around us, while cognitive distortions are the patterns of thinking that reinforce those beliefs. While limiting beliefs can lead to cognitive distortions, cognitive distortions can also create or reinforce limiting beliefs.

Cognitive Distortions: When Thinking Goes Awry

- Magnifying/Minimizing: This distortion exaggerates negative aspects while downplaying positive ones. Obsessing over minor mistakes while ignoring accomplishments can lead to feelings of worthlessness.
- Catastrophizing: Jumping to the worst possible outcome, even in unlikely scenarios, characterizes this distortion.
- Overgeneralization: A single negative event snowballs into a broad negative belief about oneself or the world, such as "I'm a failure and will never succeed."
- Magical Thinking: This distortion involves believing that thoughts or actions can unrealistically control external events. For instance, thinking positive thoughts alone will ensure success.
- Personalization: Assuming unfounded responsibility for events beyond one's control, like blaming oneself for a friend's bad mood, can lead to guilt and anxiety.
- Jumping to Conclusions: Making assumptions without evidence can fuel unnecessary conflict or emotional distress. For example, assuming a partner is upset without asking can lead to arguments.
- Emotional Reasoning: Believing that emotions always accurately reflect reality can be misleading. Feeling anxious about a presentation doesn't guarantee it will go poorly.
- Disqualifying the Positive: Brushing aside compliments or positive experiences can distort one's sense of self-worth. Dismissing praise as insincere can be an example.
- "Should" Statements: Imposing rigid expectations on oneself or others can foster guilt and frustration.
- Black and White Thinking: Viewing situations in extremes (good/bad, right/wrong) can hinder compromise and problem-solving, straining relationships.

Changing the Narrative

At some point in your life, you may have found yourself questioning, "Why me? Why am I the scapegoat? What is wrong with me? What did I do to deserve this? Why does my parent hate me so much?" It's essential to reframe these thoughts. It's not about any inadequacy or flaw that you might have. Your imperfections were never meant to justify abuse. No healthy parent would ever scapegoat their own child.

You possess a multitude of powerful qualities such as strength of character, beauty, talents, charisma, authenticity, popularity, or bravery. These attributes may trigger the narcissist's own sense of inadequacy, leading them to feel threatened by you.

The narcissistic parent's tactic is to deflect attention away from our qualities by turning them into flaws. They do this to keep you weak and prevent you from embracing your light, knowing that if you do, you will outshine them.

Though we often underestimate our own strength, the narcissist recognizes the power we possess. They attempt to isolate us, manipulate others into perceiving our qualities as major flaws, and twist instances where we stood up for ourselves into false accusations and manipulative lies.

The problem lies not in our capabilities but in our failure to recognize our own worth which is what the narcissist wants. This is what prevents us from tapping into our true inner power.

The narcissist's behavior merely reflects their own self-hatred. They resent us for refusing to become extensions of them, for questioning their distorted views, and for refusing to part with our authenticity. By not accepting their distorted views and by refusing to conform to their wishes, we become a threat to their fragile ego.

Ultimately they cannot handle the emotions that our light stirs within their hearts.

The Strength Within: Reframing the Scapegoat's Character

Children scapegoated in narcissistic families often possess a unique blend of traits. Strength of will, empathy, and a desire for justice might be seen as weaknesses in this dysfunctional environment. However, these are the very qualities that define their inner strength and resilience.

Let's celebrate the positive qualities that make you the beautiful person that you really are:

- Determination and Persistence: What may appear as stubbornness is in fact your steadfast commitment to achieving your goals. Your persistence serves as an essential quality for success.

- Ambition and Drive: Despite being perceived as a threat to the narcissistic parent's ego, your drive is in fact a testament to your strength and potential.

- Sense of Justice and Integrity: Refusing to tolerate manipulative or exploitative behavior, you embody integrity and morality. Your strong sense of justice guides you towards making ethical decisions that align with your values.

- Resilience and Adaptability: While resilience may challenge the parent's own sense of victimhood, it showcases your ability to bounce back and surmount obstacles. Your adaptability enables you to flourish amidst changing circumstances.

- Assertiveness and Self-Advocacy: Your courage to confront abuse or mistreatment demonstrates a profound strength in standing up for yourself and making choices in line with your values. Your assertiveness reflects your inner fortitude.

These qualities are not flaws, but rather triumphs and reflections of your inner resilience. Let us celebrate and honor these traits, recognizing that they contribute to your unique power and individuality.

The Meaning of Failure for the Scapegoat

As the designated family scapegoat, you have faced many setbacks and disappointments throughout your life, which have been amplified by a parent using your failures as evidence of their own righteousness and your inadequacy. Bearing the weight of these experiences can be challenging, and it is easy to lose sight of your goals and feel like giving up. However, it is important to remember that failure is not a measure of your worth as a person; it is simply a part of the learning process.

A narcissistic parent may have instilled in you a fear of failure by conditioning you to believe that your worth as a person is directly tied to your failures. They may have used your mistakes as a means of control or manipulation, pressuring you to abandon your own aspirations in favor of theirs. Failure was often used as a weapon, with love, affection, and validation withheld, criticism doled out, and guilt and shame used as tools to keep you in line.

In the real world beyond the toxic teachings instilled in you by your narcissist parent, failure is in fact, an inevitable part of life. It is a natural part of the learning and growth process, and it is through failure that we gain valuable experience and knowledge. Rather than seeing failure as something to be feared, it should be embraced as an opportunity to learn and grow. Success is not the absence of failure, but rather the ability to adapt, learn, and grow from failure.

Failure is not an end, but a new beginning. It is a learning opportunity to shed what doesn't work and amplify what does. Use it as a stepping stone, a guide, and a teacher on your journey to achieving your goals. Failure may even lead to new discoveries and paths that were previously hidden from you. Every failure is a chance for growth and learning.

Reframing your relationship with failure and your mindset about self-perception is a powerful tool that can positively impact your personal growth and development. It involves changing the way you view yourself, specific experiences, or situations by shifting your perspective and focusing on the opportunities for growth and learning rather than the setbacks.

Tips and Tricks To Vanquish Limiting Beliefs

Separate Yourself From Your Thoughts

A helpful exercise is to acknowledge and write down these negative thoughts as they arise. Try using the following steps:

1. Write down the thought: "I noticed that I had the thought that..."
2. Follow it up with the negative thought that you noticed.
3. Take a moment to read what you wrote out loud and

acknowledge the thought.

By bringing these negative thoughts to the surface, you are giving yourself the opportunity to challenge and reframe them. You may be surprised to see how frequently these thoughts occur and how they may be affecting your actions and decisions.

Not all thoughts that cross my mind are true, just as not all thoughts that cross yours are true.

Think of a green sky with hearts floating in the air instead of clouds. Did my statement conjure up such an image in your mind? Does it mean that it's true?

Cognitive Restructuring

Cognitive restructuring can help you overcome negative and irrational thoughts by identifying them and replacing them with more realistic and positive thoughts. By following the steps of cognitive restructuring, you can learn to gain a more balanced perspective on your thoughts and feelings.

1. Start by identifying the negative thought that is causing you distress. In this case, it might be the thought that "Everyone is talking behind my back and saying bad things about me."

2. Ask yourself whether there is any evidence that supports this negative thought or whether there is evidence that contradicts it. For example, have you actually heard people talking about you, or are you simply assuming that they are?

3. Consider alternative explanations for the situation. For instance, maybe the people you thought were talking about you were actually discussing something else entirely.

4. Think about how this negative thought is affecting you. For example, it might be making you feel anxious, paranoid, or self-conscious.

5. Finally, replace the negative thought with a more positive and realistic one. For example, instead of thinking "Everyone is talking behind my back," you could reframe your thought as "I don't have any concrete proof that people are talking about me, and

even if they are, I can choose to focus on my positive relationships and not let this situation consume me."

Questions to Challenge Thoughts That Hinder Personal Growth

1. What is the worry that is stopping you from going forward?
2. How likely is it that the worry will come true?
3. If the worry comes true, what is the worst that will happen?
4. If the worry doesn't come true, what will most likely happen?
5. If the worry comes true, what are the chances that you will be ok: In one week_____% In one Month_____% In one Year_____%

Positive Reframing

Positive reframing is a technique that involves changing the way you think about a situation or thought by focusing on the positive aspects, rather than the negative ones. The purpose of positive reframing is to shift your perspective from negative to positive, which can help to reduce negative thoughts and feelings.

Here's an exercise that utilizes positive reframing:

1. Start by identifying a negative thought that you frequently have. For example, "I'm not good enough for this job."
2. Reframe the negative thought to focus on the positive aspects you identified. For example, "I may not have all the skills yet, but I have a lot of passion for this field. With hard work and dedication, I can learn and grow in this job."
3. Practice saying the reframed thought to yourself regularly, and reinforce it with positive self-talk. For example, "I'm excited to take on this challenge and learn as much as I can."

Decatastrophizing

Decatastrophizing is a cognitive-behavioral technique that helps to reduce the negative thoughts and emotions associated with catastrophic thinking. For example, let's say that you feel like others are talking behind your back. In such a scenario it can be easy to jump to catastrophic conclusions and assume the worst. However, by using decatastrophizing, you can challenge these negative thoughts and develop a more balanced perspective.

Here is an exercise that you can use to practice decatastrophizing:

1. Start by identifying the catastrophic thought that is bothering you. In this case, it might be "Everyone is talking behind my back and saying bad things about me."
2. Consider the worst possible outcome of this thought. For example, "Everyone will hate me and I will be completely alone."
3. Write down any evidence that supports or refutes the catastrophic thought. For example, you might write down evidence that supports the thought, such as "I heard people whispering when I walked by." You might also write down evidence that refutes the thought, such as "I have no concrete proof that anyone is talking behind my back."
4. Consider alternative explanations for the situation. For example, maybe the people you heard whispering were talking about something unrelated to you.
5. Use the evidence and alternative explanations to develop a new, balanced thought that is more realistic and less catastrophic. For example, "I don't have any concrete evidence that people are talking behind my back, and even if they are, it's not the end of the world. I can choose to focus on the positive relationships in my life and not let this situation consume me."

Journal Prompts

- What beliefs do I hold about myself that might be holding me back?

- What beliefs do I have about success and failure that might be limiting me?
- What beliefs do I hold about money and abundance that might be limiting my ability to achieve financial success?
- What beliefs do I have about relationships and love that might be limiting my ability to find and maintain healthy relationships?
- What beliefs do I hold about my capabilities and skills that might be limiting my potential?
- What fears or anxieties do I have that might be rooted in limiting beliefs?
- What assumptions do I make about the world and the people around me that might be limiting my growth?
- What negative self-talk or critical inner dialogue do I engage in that might be rooted in limiting beliefs?
- When faced with a challenge or obstacle, what thoughts or beliefs tend to hold me back rather than propel me forward?
- What would I do differently if I didn't believe these limiting thoughts or beliefs?

The Lessons Learned

Limiting beliefs can act as invisible chains, holding us back from reaching our full potential. The good news is, we have the power to break free. Overcoming these beliefs requires becoming an active participant in shaping our own lives, taking responsibility for our thoughts and actions, and committing to self-improvement.

The first step is becoming aware of the negative self-talk that fuels limiting beliefs. Pay attention to the inner critic whispering doubts and fears. Ask yourself, "Is this thought truly serving me?" Often, these thoughts are based on unfounded assumptions or past experiences that don't define your present or future.

Challenge negative thoughts by replacing them with empowering affirmations that align with your values and goals. Instead of "I'm not good enough," try "I am capable and worthy of success." Visualize yourself achieving your goals and overcoming challenges. These mental exercises can help solidify your new beliefs.

Recognize patterns within your upbringing that might have contributed to these beliefs. With self-compassion, understand that you can choose to break free from these cycles and create new, healthier patterns for yourself.

Overcoming limiting beliefs is a journey, not a destination. Be patient with yourself, celebrate your victories, and embrace the growth mindset. By actively challenging negative thoughts and nurturing positive beliefs, you can unlock your full potential and create a life filled with purpose and fulfillment.

Chapter 16

Honor Your Sacred Self

You are Sacred.

You are here, you are a part of this world, you are a part of the universal energy, the breath of life flows through you, and the fact that you exist exactly as you are, right now, makes you sacred.

When we think of the word sacred, we think of something or someone that we respect, that we honor, someone who is blessed and worthy of our reverence. Something sacred is not something that needs to be perfect or flawless. In fact, sacred things rarely are.

Think of a little stone that one may have picked up as they were on a pilgrimage and found themselves on spiritual ground. Do you think that the stone's shape would be perfect? Or could that stone be chipped, may be an odd shape, may not have a particularly interesting color, and may be gray just like the rest of them? This is highly likely. But because it was picked up on sacred ground, this rock holds special significance and is deemed sacred by the pilgrim who safeguards it.

What would happen if you began to treat yourself with this narrative in mind? What if you would safeguard yourself in the same way?

Despite the obstacles that you have had to and still have to overcome, despite the issues that you are still battling with, doesn't change the fact that you are worthy of living a life of joy and peace. You are worthy to treat yourself as the sacred being that you really are.

Therefore, treating yourself like you matter makes sense under this light. Does it not? Do you make decisions for yourself based on the sole belief that you matter? Do you make empowering decisions that strengthen you? Do you protect yourself and nurture yourself? Do your thoughts and beliefs about yourself support you? If the answer is "no," it is time for you to shift your thoughts.

You will regain your sense of purpose and power when you tend to your spirit. you will find yourself when you begin respecting your inherent goodness, and your true nature.

The problem is that your difficult journey may have led you to lose touch with who you really are. We tend to overidentify with our difficulties.

When we know we are sacred, without a shadow of a doubt, we stand taller in the face of challenges because we know that we are not our problems. We know that at our core, we deserve to hold our rightful space in this world. Yes, you may have fallen several times, but you got back up each time because you know that this is not the end of the story just as it isn't the end of mine.

Honor and respect the sacred within you. Honor and respect the sacred around you. Honor and respect the sacred that carries you. It will get you through the tough times. It always has for me.

Your Sacred Space

A sacred space is a place or state where one can feel safe, free to exist within one's authenticity, and liberated from criticism and external pressures. It serves as an environment for self-discovery, self-care, and self-expression. Such spaces can be found in physical locations that feel safe to you, in your mind and spirit, which are yours and yours alone, and in your physical body, which is the temple that carries your spirit.

The power of honoring your sacred spaces is immense, as it serves as a cocoon that envelops you, keeps you safe, repels negative energy, and guides you along your journey.

Your sacred space is your spiritual sanctuary, where

you are valuable, important, and deserving of love and care. It's a place where you prioritize yourself, and where your feelings, thoughts, and preferences take precedence. This is the space that you hold within yourself to experience your emotions, to contemplate your thoughts, and to fully express yourself without fear of judgment or criticism, celebrating your uniqueness and authenticity.

Honoring your sacred space is an act of self-love and self-respect, reflecting your personality, values, connections, safety, and self-honoring. It serves as a tangible reminder that your life is your own. It's where you can connect with yourself on a deeper level, find peace and comfort amidst the chaos of the world, and cultivate inner tranquility.

Your Environmental Sacred Space

Your environmental sacred space is a unique area in your surroundings that you designate as sacred and conducive to your well-being. It could be a physical location in nature, such as a quiet forest grove, your favorite waterside spot, or a secluded field where you can retreat and be alone. It can be the space you inhabit daily, whether it's a specific room in your home, a cozy nook where you can wrap yourself in a blanket, or a place designated for your creative endeavors, like the kitchen or garage.

This space is defined by its ability to facilitate personal growth, creativity, learning, goal-setting, and self-expression. It's a place where you can be yourself, embrace your uniqueness, and cultivate feelings of peace, tranquility, and connection with your inner self. Depending on your spiritual inclinations, you may choose to adorn it with elements like plants, crystals, candles, or meaningful artwork. Alternatively, if you require this space to be a place for grounding yourself, you might surround yourself with inspiring quotes, figures that you admire, and items that reflect your passions and aspirations.

Ultimately, your environmental sacred space serves as a refuge from the demands of everyday life, providing you with a sanctuary to recharge, reflect, and reconnect with your inner essence. Creating and maintaining this space requires intentionality and mindfulness, as you must dedicate time and energy to cultivate an environment that nurtures your spiritual and emotional well-being. By honoring and tending to your environmental sacred space, you can foster a deeper sense of harmony, balance, and connection with yourself.

Setting an Intention

Creating a sacred space isn't just about designing a physical area; it's also about setting an intention and cultivating a mindset of self-care and respect. Before entering your sacred space, take off your shoes, keep it clean and tidy, and give it the respect that it deserves. After all, this is the place that embodies safety and will provide solace after a long day. Whatever your intention may be, take a moment to appreciate this sacred space, take a deep breath, and set the tone for your experience.

A personal space designated for self-care, peace, and safety is essential for your mental and emotional well-being. It's not simply a space where you journal about gratitude, although this is a great practice to uphold, but also about prioritizing your needs and giving yourself the attention you deserve. Taking the time to listen to your body, relax, and enjoy the present moment can make a significant difference in your overall quality of life.

To ensure that your sacred space is a safe and secure place, it's important to establish boundaries and rules. These rules can vary depending on your individual needs, but some examples include only allowing emotionally safe people to enter, avoiding any toxic gifts or letters that may have been sent your way, and keeping any objects that remind you of negative experiences or people out of the area. This rule is very important, and you may even want to avoid looking at potentially triggering emails or scrolling through potentially triggering social media in the area if you can help it.

Taking the time to reflect on what makes you feel safe and secure and incorporating those elements into your sacred space will help you on those days when you may feel overwhelmed by emotions or may have been triggered by something or someone. If you consistently utilize your sacred space as intended, it will offer relief and a feeling of safety when you enter it. It will serve as a space that empowers you to make good decisions, a place where you can rest, and a place where you can prioritize your needs above anyone else's.

Nature's Sacredness

Exposure to nature offers a multitude of benefits. Sunlight warms our skin, fresh air supports immune system function and overall health, and the calming presence of plants reduces stress and boosts mood.

Inviting nature in, and making it a part of our healing journey isn't just about aesthetics; it's a portal to a deeper sense of well-being. Studies show that simply looking at natural scenery lowers blood pressure and reduces anxiety. Houseplants not only purify the air but also offer a sense of companionship and a reminder of the vibrant life force that surrounds us.

Weaving nature into your sacred space can take many forms. Perhaps it's a meditation corner adorned with nature photographs or a cozy reading nook near a window. Maybe it's a commitment to spending time in nature each day.

Let nature be your guide. Start small with a single plant, open a window to embrace the fresh air, or place a bowl of smooth stones on your altar. Every step you take to connect with the natural world enhances the power and serenity of your sacred space.

The Sanctum Within

Unlike the physical world, constantly evolving, with objects being replaced to make room for new ones, with ever-evolving creations and time making the new become old, and the old dissolving, the inner landscape holds a unique kind of sanctuary – as it is not bound to the erosions of time. This sacred space, untouched by external circumstances, is a wellspring of peace and a refuge from life's storms. Ancient wisdom traditions across cultures speak of this inner haven, often using metaphors like "the still point within" or "the chamber of the heart."

Modern science is starting to catch up. Research on

mindfulness and meditation reveals the quieting of the amygdala (the brain's fear center) and the activation of the prefrontal cortex (associated with focus and emotional regulation) during these practices. These findings suggest that accessing the sanctum within can have a tangible impact on our well-being.

Unlocking this inner sanctum is always within your power, as you do not need to spend money or rely on any external factor at all. It is all within you. You can bring your focus to your breath, feeling the rise and fall of your chest or abdomen. As thoughts arise, acknowledge them gently and return your focus to your breath. With practice, this anchors you in the present moment and creates a space for inner peace.

And as you do this, you can let your imagination guide you to find your sacred sanctum. Is it a sun-drenched beach, a quiet forest clearing, or a majestic mountain peak? Engage all your senses. Imagine the warmth of the sun on your skin, the smell the fresh air as you listen to the sound of waves or birdsong. The more vivid the visualization, the easier it becomes to access this inner space.

Even a few minutes of daily meditation, allowing yourself to escape into your mind's peaceful and safe space, can strengthen your ability to access this inner haven, fostering resilience and calm amidst life's challenges.

Unveiling the Sanctum: Facing the Guardian at the Gate

The journey inward isn't always smooth sailing. Sometimes, as you approach the threshold of your sanctum, you might encounter a formidable obstacle – inner resistance. This resistance can manifest in various ways.

You might feel a sudden urge to fidget, check your phone, or clean the house – anything to avoid the stillness of meditation. Long-suppressed emotions might bubble to the surface, making you want to retreat from the introspection. A critical inner voice might tell you you're "bad at meditating" or that "nothing will come of this." This negativity can discourage you from continuing.These are all normal experiences. The key is to approach them with compassion and awareness.

During this process, it is important to acknowledge

your Feelings. Instead of pushing away your resistance, acknowledge its presence. Simply notice the restlessness, the emotions, or the self-doubt without judgment. Label them as "restlessness" or "critical thoughts" and observe them with detachment. Remember, it takes courage to explore your inner world. If your mind wanders, gently guide your attention back to your chosen technique, like focusing on your breath or a mantra.

Think of your inner resistance as a guardian at the gate of your sanctum. This guardian might seem intimidating at first, but by acknowledging its presence and approaching it with gentleness, you can navigate your way past.

With consistent practice and a compassionate approach, you can overcome these initial hurdles and unlock the peace and serenity that awaits you within your sanctum.

Your Physical Sacred Space

We might not always be fully aware or fully connected to the physical space our conscious minds inhabit – our body – a temple worthy of reverence and care. Ancient wisdom traditions across cultures have emphasized this connection between body and mind. Just as we cultivate a sacred space within, we must also prioritize the well-being of our physical vessel.

Your body has carried you through everything that you have ever been through. It is the most important witness to the whole story of you. It is the gateway between your mind and the physical environment that you inhabit. Through our bodies, we interact with the world, experience joy and sorrow, and forge connections with others. It's the vehicle that allows us to navigate life's journey. The physical body provides a foundation for the inner sanctuary. When our physical health is compromised, it can be more difficult to access the peace and clarity of the sanctum. The way we treat our bodies often reflects our inner state. Prioritizing self-care nourishes not just the physical but also the emotional and spiritual aspects of ourselves.

Honoring Your Temple is a gateway to your inner world and environment. Your body is an instrument that can be used to calm your mind, to bring you closer to your goals, and to connect you with the world around you.

Self-Soothing Techniques

- Self-hug: Wrap your arms around yourself and give yourself a gentle squeeze, as if you're giving yourself a hug. You can also rock back and forth slightly while hugging yourself.
- Hand on heart: Place one or both hands over your heart center, which is located in the center of your chest. Close your eyes and take a few deep breaths, feeling the warmth and pressure of your hands on your chest.
- Grounding touch: Touch a part of your body that feels solid and grounding, such as your thighs, feet, or hands. Focus on the sensation of your touch and the connection between your body and the ground.
- Somatic tracking: Scan your body from head to toe, noticing any areas of tension, discomfort, or pain. Use your hands to gently touch and explore these areas, allowing yourself to fully feel and acknowledge the sensations without judgment.
- Abdominal breathing: Place one hand on your belly and take slow, deep breaths, focusing on the rise and fall of your abdomen. This can help regulate your breathing and calm your nervous system.

Exercises That Are Commonly Recommended for Releasing Trauma

- Yoga: Yoga is a great way to release tension and stress from the body. It can help to calm the nervous system and promote relaxation. Certain poses, such as child's pose or downward facing dog, can be particularly effective for releasing trapped energy.
- Running: Running or jogging is a high-intensity exercise that can help to release endorphins and reduce stress levels. It can also help to release tension from the muscles and promote a feeling of relaxation.

- Dancing: Dancing is a great way to move the body and release trapped energy. It can help to promote a feeling of joy and freedom, and can be particularly effective for those who have experienced trauma related to the body.

- Boxing: Boxing or martial arts can be an effective way to release pent-up anger and frustration. It can also help to build strength and confidence.

- Swimming: Swimming is a low-impact exercise that can be very soothing for the body. It can help to release tension from the muscles and promote a feeling of relaxation.

- Tai Chi: Tai Chi is a gentle form of exercise that involves slow, flowing movements. It can be particularly effective for promoting relaxation and reducing stress levels.

- Breathwork: Breathwork exercises, such as deep breathing or pranayama, can be very effective for releasing tension from the body and calming the nervous system.

- Meditation: Meditation can help to promote a sense of calm and relaxation, and can be particularly effective for those who have experienced trauma related to the mind and emotions.

Remember, everyone's body is different, and it's important to find an exercise or movement practice that feels safe and comfortable for you.

Honoring Your Body Through Healthy Routines

- Get enough sleep: Getting enough sleep is crucial for overall health and well-being. Aim for 7-8 hours of sleep per night to help your body and mind recover.

- Practice relaxation techniques: Incorporating relaxation techniques such as deep breathing, meditation, or yoga into your daily routine can help reduce stress and promote a sense of calm.

- Eat a healthy diet: Eating a healthy diet that includes plenty of fruits, vegetables, lean proteins, and whole grains can help nourish your body and improve your mood.

- Drink plenty of water: Staying hydrated is important for maintaining good health. Aim for at least 8 glasses of water per day to help flush out toxins and keep your body functioning properly.
- Practice good hygiene: Practicing good hygiene, such as washing your hands regularly and brushing your teeth twice a day, can help prevent illness and promote overall health.
- Take breaks: It's important to take breaks throughout the day to rest and recharge. Whether it's taking a short walk outside or simply sitting quietly for a few minutes, giving yourself permission to take a break can help reduce stress and improve your overall well-being.

You Are What You Eat

Eating nutrient-dense foods, such as fruits, vegetables, whole grains, lean proteins, and healthy fats can have a positive impact on your emotional well-being. These foods provide the body with essential nutrients that can help to reduce feelings of anxiety and improve mood.

There Are a Variety of Foods That Are Known to Help with Anxiety, Including:

- Omega-3 fatty acids: Foods rich in omega-3 fatty acids, such as fatty fish (salmon, mackerel, sardines), flaxseeds, chia seeds, and walnuts, have anti-inflammatory effects that can help to reduce symptoms of anxiety.
- Probiotics: Foods that contain probiotics, such as yogurt, kefir, sauerkraut, and kimchi, can help to improve gut health and support the immune system, which in turn can help to reduce anxiety.
- Tryptophan-rich foods: Foods that are rich in tryptophan, an amino acid that is a precursor to serotonin, a neurotransmitter that regulates mood, include turkey, eggs, cheese, and nuts.
- Magnesium-rich foods: Magnesium is known to have a calming effect on the body and can be found in

foods such as spinach, pumpkin seeds, yogurt, black beans, and avocado.

- Vitamin B-rich foods: Vitamin B6, in particular, plays a role in the production of neurotransmitters and can be found in foods such as chickpeas, tuna, turkey, and chicken.
- Complex Carbohydrates: Eating complex carbohydrates such as whole grains, fruits and vegetables can help to boost levels of serotonin, a neurotransmitter that regulates mood

Using Your Body to Release Thoughts and Emotions

Creative expression can be an important tool for releasing trauma because it you to express yourself in a nonverbal way. Trauma can be difficult to articulate, and traditional forms of talk therapy may not always be effective for everyone. Creative expression can provide a way to communicate emotions and experiences that are too overwhelming or painful to put into words.

Creative expression also engages the right side of the brain, which is responsible for processing emotions, sensory information, and nonverbal communication. When a person creates art, music, or writing, they tap into this part of the brain and can access emotions and experiences that may be difficult to access through talking alone.

Additionally, creative expression can provide a sense of control and empowerment. Through the process of creation, one can take ownership of their experiences and create something positive out of a negative situation.

There are many ways that one can go about the process of self-expression.

- Body mapping: Using a large piece of paper, you can lie down and trace your body onto the paper. Then, color in different parts of your body to represent different emotions or sensations you are feeling. This can help you to identify areas of tension or discomfort in your body and regulate your emotional response.
- Drawing emotions: Draw or paint what your emotions feel like in your body. This can help you to

externalize internal experiences and regulate emotional responses. It can also help you to gain a better understanding of your emotional state and promote emotional regulation.
- Collage: Create a collage that represents a safe and calming place. This can be a helpful tool for grounding and self-soothing during times of distress. It can also provide a sense of comfort and safety when you are feeling overwhelmed.
- Mandala creation: Mandala creation involves drawing or coloring a circular pattern. This can be a meditative exercise that can help to calm your nervous system. The repetitive nature of the pattern can help to induce a sense of relaxation and reduce feelings of anxiety or stress.
- Freeform art: Allow yourself to create any kind of art you want without any constraints or guidelines. This can be a way to express yourself creatively and release emotional tension. It can also provide a sense of empowerment and self-expression.

Journal Prompts

- What does a sacred space mean to you? How would you define it environmentally, physically and spiritually?
- What are the potential obstacles that might prevent you from creating your sacred space? Write down the challenges and how you plan to overcome them.
- What do you need to do to prepare your chosen location for your sacred space? Write down the steps you need to take, such as uncluttering, cleaning, or decorating.
- How do you want to maintain your sacred space? Write down the rituals or practices that you want to do to keep it energetically clean and charged.

Lessons Learned

Committing to your self-care routines as non-negotiable means integrating them into your daily life as indispensable rituals, much like eating or sleeping. This entails a deliberate and unwavering dedication to self-care practices, even amidst competing demands or distractions. By steadfastly prioritizing self-care, you affirm the significance of your well-being and healing, acknowledging your inherent worthiness of time and attention.

Your self-care routines serve as a testament to the sanctity within you, nurturing and honoring your sacred essence. Moreover, upholding these routines establishes healthy boundaries and bolsters self-respect, empowering you to assert control over your life and prioritize your own needs and desires. Embracing self-care as non-negotiable fosters a sense of stability and resilience, equipping you to navigate life's challenges with greater ease and grace.

Chapter 17

Finding Happiness

Finding happiness may feel like a foreign concept at first for those of us who grew up in dysfunctional family dynamics where our agency to be happy was consistently compromised. However, it is something that can indeed happen, and it is something worth striving for and working towards, even though we may not always believe it to be possible.

In my own healing process, I encountered feelings of guilt when I began to feel better. It was a peculiar space to navigate because as I started to feel better, I questioned myself for having left the narcissistic family system. Feeling better made me question whether I was really abused. Shouldn't I feel irreversibly damaged? And then, I would find myself caught in loops where I needed to revisit memories, journals, and remind myself of everything that happened. It became a vicious cycle. I had to realize that I was sabotaging my own happiness. I wasn't giving myself permission to finally start living my life. And the truth was that I didn't really know how to do it, or what I needed.

And so, it dawned on me that maybe I did need to revisit my past, but not by looking at what they took away from me, but rather looking at what it was that I needed and was never given so that I may begin the process of giving those things to myself.

Meeting Your Own Needs Without Feeling Guilty About It

A need refers to a requirement or necessity essential for a person's well-being, growth, or survival. Needs can encompass various aspects of life, including physical, emotional, social, and psychological requirements.

Maslow's Hierarchy of Needs, developed by Abraham Maslow, is a psychological theory presented in the form of a pyramid. It can be perceived as a ladder of human motivation, with each step building upon the one below. At the pyramid's base are fundamental needs like air and shelter, forming the foundation. As these basic needs are met, one can ascend to higher levels, seeking safety, social connections, recognition, and, ultimately, self-actualization – the realization of personal potential. This structure suggests that people generally progress through these stages sequentially, aiming to fulfill one level before moving to the next. However, real-life experiences often involve navigating multiple needs simultaneously, and one may revisit lower levels if certain needs remain unmet.

Over time, Maslow's Hierarchy of Needs has evolved as researchers and psychologists have expanded upon and critiqued the original model. While the core concepts remain relevant, some modifications and additions have been made to reflect a more nuanced understanding of human motivation and well-being. For example, Maslow later introduced aesthetic needs, highlighting the importance of beauty and balance in human experience. Additionally, the concept of cognitive needs, involving the desire for knowledge and understanding, was incorporated to emphasize the role of intellectual stimulation in personal growth. Furthermore, the notion of self-transcendence was added to acknowledge the pursuit of connection to something greater than oneself, such as spirituality or altruism, as a fundamental aspect of human fulfillment.

Maslow's Hierarchy of Needs provides a holistic perspective on human motivation and well-being.

Maslow's Hierarchy Of Needs

- Physiological Needs: This forms the foundation of Maslow's hierarchy, encompassing basic necessities for survival like air, water, food, shelter, and sleep.

- Safety Needs: Once physiological needs are met, the next step is seeking safety and security. This includes physical safety, health, financial stability, and protection from accidents or harm, providing predictability and control in one's life.

- Love and Belongingness Needs: The third level involves social needs, such as forming interpersonal relationships, feeling a sense of belonging, love, and acceptance. These connections contribute to emotional well-being and are crucial for overall mental health.

- Esteem Needs: Esteem needs involve gaining a sense of self-worth and recognition from others. This includes achieving personal goals, gaining respect, and feeling competent and confident. Both internal and external recognition play a role in fulfilling esteem needs.

- Self-Actualization Needs: Self-actualization represents the realization of one's full potential and capabilities. This involves personal growth, creativity, problem-solving, and the pursuit of fulfilling one's unique talents and abilities.

- Aesthetic Needs: Aesthetic needs emphasize the importance of beauty, balance, and form. This level involves the appreciation of art, nature, and other aesthetically pleasing experiences, contributing to a more holistic sense of well-being.

- Cognitive Needs: Cognitive needs involve the desire for knowledge, understanding, and exploration. This includes intellectual stimulation, curiosity, and the pursuit of meaningful learning experiences, contributing to personal growth and a deeper understanding of the world.

- Self-Transcendence: Self-transcendence, goes beyond a person's self. It involves a sense of connection to something greater than oneself, such as spirituality, altruism, or a higher purpose. This level suggests that true fulfillment comes from transcending personal concerns and contributing to the greater good.

Understanding the Fundamental Unmet Needs of the Family Scapegoat

Even in healthy families, children's emotional needs may encounter challenges due to life's fluctuations and unpredictability, such as sickness or divorce. No one is entirely immune from the experience of having unmet needs during their upbringing. However, the primary focus here is to delve into the process of healing from the aftermath of surviving scapegoating.

Within a narcissistic family system, a scapegoated child's understanding of fundamental needs becomes distorted, creating a profound disconnection from their own needs as they transition into adulthood.

For example, essential provisions like shelter and being fed are manipulated as bargaining chips, exploiting the absence of acknowledgment for deeper emotional needs such as connection, understanding, security, and acceptance. Within these households, the scapegoat's longing to be seen, heard, cherished, and to feel emotionally safe, are completely ignored, invalidated, and tossed under the rug, labeled as 'irrational tantrums for attention.' They are often guilt-tripped for even expressing such needs, made to feel that their emotional needs are irrational and that they should harbor a sense of guilt for daring to voice such demands, especially considering the provision of food and shelter they already receive.

The scapegoat is inundated with messages like "you're provided for, stop complaining" or "you should be grateful for what you have." Additionally, they may be told, "your needs for love and acceptance are not met because of your character," fostering a belief that their intrinsic needs are unworthy or excessive. This continual messaging perpetuates the notion that seeking emotional fulfillment is an unreasonable demand.

The healing journey begins with understanding and acknowledging our own needs, paving the way for self-fulfillment and genuine growth.

Breaking free from this cycle requires recognizing our own ability to meet our needs. Instead of seeking validation and acceptance from others, we can nurture self-acceptance and cultivate a healthy connection with ourselves.

- Physiological Needs: Begin by tending to your immediate physical needs, such as health and nutrition. Establishing a stable foundation allows you to focus on higher-level needs.

- Safety Needs: Create a sense of safety by recognizing and setting personal boundaries. Seeking therapy or counseling can be instrumental in processing past traumas and contributing to emotional security.

- Belongingness and Love Needs: Cultivate supportive relationships outside your family circle, creating a network of understanding and acceptance. Engage in group activities or communities that align with your personal interests for a sense of belonging.

- Esteem Needs: Challenge negative self-perceptions through therapy or self-reflection. Acknowledge and celebrate your personal accomplishments, fostering a positive self-image and boosting self-esteem.

- Self-Actualization: Identify and pursue personal interests and goals that align with your passions. Seek educational opportunities or skill development to foster personal growth and fulfillment.

- Aesthetic Needs: Engage in activities that bring you joy and appreciation for beauty. Surround yourself with aesthetically pleasing environments to contribute to a positive mindset.

- Cognitive Needs: Pursue continuous learning and self-discovery through education and exploration. Challenge your mind with intellectually stimulating activities or discussions to enhance cognitive well-being.

- Self-Transcendence: Explore activities or pursuits that provide a deeper sense of purpose and connection beyond yourself. This might involve contributing to a cause, volunteering, or engaging in activities that promote the well-being of others.

A Need Is Not to Be Confused with a Want

A need is essential for our survival and fundamental to our emotional and physical health. On the other hand, a want is a desire for immediate gratification, often fueled by our impulses and sensory cravings.

While wants may provide temporary pleasure, they are not sustainable sources of happiness and contentment. In fact, focusing solely on our wants can lead to a never-ending cycle of seeking pleasure and never finding true fulfillment. Wants, such as indulging in unhealthy habits like overeating, excessive drinking or substance abuse, can harm our well-being and negatively impact our lives.

What are some examples of wants?
- A new car
- A bigger house
- A luxurious vacation
- The latest smartphone
- Designer clothing
- Expensive jewelry

It's important to remember that wants are fleeting, whereas our needs are the foundation of our well-being. Focusing on our needs, rather than our wants, helps us cultivate a strong sense of self-awareness and inner peace.

Tending To Your Inner Child

The inner child refers to the emotional and psychological aspect of ourselves that is connected to our childhood experiences and emotions. It is the part of ourselves that holds memories, beliefs, and emotions that were formed in childhood and may still influence our thoughts and behavior in adulthood. The inner child can be seen as the emotional and psychological equivalent of our physical childhood self. It is often associated with feelings of innocence, vulnerability, and emotional openness. Connecting with the inner child can help us to understand and process our past experiences, improve self-awareness and emotional intelligence, and create more fulfilling relationships.

Connecting with our inner child can be a difficult process for many of us, as it often involves acknowledging and grieving the loss of the childhood and teenagehood that we needed but didn't receive. It's about rediscovering the parts of ourselves that we've forgotten and reconnecting with the parts of ourselves that were never given the opportunity to exist. It's also about learning to fulfill the needs that we didn't even know we had.

As we grow into adulthood, our younger selves don't simply disappear. Our younger selves, including the toddler, child, and teenager, still exist within us. These parts of ourselves are at different stages and have different experiences and needs. Many of us are unaware that our triggers are, in fact, the younger versions of ourselves crying out for attention.

A part of us may still believe that we are not able to express our emotions, that our unique character traits and talents are bad, and that we are not capable of achieving our dreams.

We need to let them know that we are in charge now, that we are free, and that we get to decide what is best for us from now on.

Learning to Play

The good news is that incorporating play is easier than you might think.

Even if you feel "too busy" or "too serious" to play, remember that play is a form of self-care. Start small – schedule 15 minutes of daily fun or brainstorm activities you enjoyed as a child. By making play a priority, you'll reap the rewards for your overall well-being.

- Rediscover old childhood hobbies: Think back to what you loved doing as a child. Did you enjoy drawing, painting, playing sports, or building with Lego? Try to pick up one of these hobbies again and allow yourself to get lost in the activity, without any pressure or expectation.

- Get physical: Engage in physical activities that allow you to let loose and have fun. Consider trying dance, trampoline jumping, or going for a bike ride. Not only are these activities good for your body, but they can also help release any built-up tension and stress.

- Play games: Games are a great way to bring playfulness into your life. You could try board games, card games, or video games. Remember to choose games that you genuinely enjoy playing, rather than games that you think you should play.

- Play with kids: Playing with children can be a great way to tap into your own inner child. Kids are naturally playful, and spending time with them can help you rediscover the joy and wonder of childhood. If you're not sure how to connect with your inner child, simply observing children at play can provide inspiration.

- If you have children of your own, allowing yourself to enter into their imaginative play can be an especially rewarding experience. Not only will it benefit you, but it can also deepen your connection with your own children.

Train Your Mind to Focus on Gratitude Instead of Shortcomings

I can empathize with the frustration of being advised to "just be grateful", as if it could somehow magically solve all of our problems and erase the trauma we've endured. In fact, this advice can serve as a painful reminder of the times when we were expected to feel grateful for receiving scraps of conditional love, often to leverage abuse, or even worse, when we were wrongly blamed for the abuse we suffered and were expected to maintain a facade of positivity despite our traumatic experiences.

However, gratitude and toxic positivity are not the same thing. It's understandable that it's hard to feel grateful when, as a survivor of your life's circumstances, at some point you've been deprived of love, safety, and dignity. But unlike toxic positivity, gratitude practice does not discount or negate your experiences. Yes, they did happen, and you must take the time to grieve your losses. But you also have the right to pursue happiness in this life and to create a peaceful future for yourself.

And you must train your mind to look for it.

Our trauma or negative life circumstances have wired our brains to focus on what's lacking, what's wrong, and what's dangerous. We must purposefully and resolutely redirect our attention towards the positive, the real, and the achievable. Why? Because by doing this, we reclaim our power back.

The power of gratitude is not just about feeling happy or content. It's about reclaiming our agency, our voice, and our worth. It's about recognizing that even in the darkest moments, there is something to be thankful for, even if it's just the fact that we have a warm bed to sleep in. It's not a cure-all, but it's a tool we can use to survive and thrive, even in the face of unspeakable pain.

To get started, try this simple exercise: think about three things that you're thankful for. These can be small things that benefit you right now - like being able to spend time outside in the sun, having a pet in your life, or feeling safe and secure in your space. The key is to focus on things that bring you joy and gratitude in your immediate environment.

Do this exercise once a week for ten weeks, and you may start to notice a shift in your mindset. Instead of dwelling on what's bringing you down, you'll be more focused on what brings you up more often than not.

It's important to note that there's no need to overdo this exercise. Doing it every day might actually backfire and make you feel like you're striving too hard for happiness. Instead, try to keep it casual and do it once a week. And if you're struggling to come up with things to be grateful for, remember that they can be simple and small. The point is to cultivate a sense of gratitude and appreciation for what's good in your life.

Keeping a mindfulness journal can also be helpful in tracking your progress and reflecting on the positive changes in your thinking patterns. So why not give it a try? With just a few minutes each week, you can start to rewire your thinking patterns and cultivate a greater sense of gratitude and well-being in your life.

Simplify Your Life

Our lives have become increasingly complex with the abundance of choices that we have at our fingertips. While it may seem like a luxury to have so many options, it can actually complicate our lives and detract from what truly matters. For example, something as simple as buying jam at the grocery store can turn into an overwhelming task, with countless brands, flavors, and ingredients to choose from.

There are two types of decision-makers: maximizers and satisficers. Maximizers are those who want to survey all of the available options before making a decision, while satisficers are content with making a quick, simple choice based on their needs and preferences. Interestingly, maximizers tend to be less happy and satisfied with their choices than satisficers.

By simplifying your life and making choices based on your own needs and preferences, you can free up mental resources and reduce decision fatigue. This can lead to a more fulfilling and satisfying life. Instead of spending hours weighing the pros and cons of every option, you can focus on what is important to you and make a decision quickly and efficiently.

Simplifying your life can also help you prioritize what truly matters. By cutting out the excess and focusing on what brings you joy and fulfillment, you can create a more meaningful life. This can involve decluttering your home, simplifying your schedule, or prioritizing your relationships and hobbies.

Overall, simplifying your life can lead to less stress, more happiness, and a greater sense of fulfillment. By reducing the complexity of your choices and focusing on what truly matters, you can create a life that is both simple and satisfying.

Random Acts of Kindness

Random acts of kindness can have a significant impact not only on the person receiving the kindness, but also on the giver. Engaging in small acts of kindness on a regular basis can create a sense of community and a feeling of interconnectedness with others. It can also help to boost your self-esteem and improve your overall mood.

It's important to remember that random acts of kindness don't have to be grand gestures. Instead, focus on small opportunities for simple acts of kindness that you can do without going beyond your comfort level. For instance, holding the door for someone, letting someone go ahead of you in line, or offering a smile or kind word to a stranger can go a long way in brightening someone's day.

Keeping track of your acts of kindness can also be a helpful way to stay motivated and see the positive impact you're making in the world. You can use a journal or a simple notepad to jot down what you did and how it made you feel.

Ultimately, the goal of random acts of kindness is to spread positivity and create a ripple effect of kindness. So, the next time you have an opportunity to do something kind for someone, take it. You never know how much it could mean to them, and how much it could brighten your own day in return.

Your Body Can Influence Your Mindset

The mind-body connection is a complex and fascinating phenomenon that has been studied by scientists and psychologists for decades. It is a two-way communication system, where the mind influences the body, and the body, in turn, affects the mind.

For instance, something as simple as smiling can have a significant impact on your mood. When you activate the muscles in your face that are used for smiling, it sends a signal to your brain that you are happy, even if you're not. This can lead to a cascade of positive emotions and help boost your mood.

Furthermore, paying attention to your posture can also influence your mindset. Standing up straight with your shoulders back and head held high can signal to your brain that you are confident and in control. This can help improve your mood and self-esteem and create a more positive mindset.

Strike Up a Friendly Conversation with a Random Person

Striking up a conversation with a stranger can seem intimidating, but it can also be an opportunity to connect with someone new and potentially brighten both of your days. Taking the time to engage in friendly conversation can help build a sense of community.

While it's important to be cautious and aware of your surroundings, there are plenty of ways to strike up a conversation in a safe and respectful manner. You might start by offering a compliment or expressing gratitude to someone who provides you with good service, such as a cashier or barista. This can help foster a positive atmosphere and make the other person feel appreciated.

Another approach might be to ask for someone's opinion or advice on a topic that you both have in common, such as a product at the store or a local event. This can be a great way to break the ice and start a conversation on a positive note.

By engaging in small friendly conversation with strangers, you can help create a more connected and positive community. Just remember to be respectful of boundaries and personal space, and to approach these interactions with an open and friendly attitude.

Choosing Happiness Doesn't Equate With Selfishness

That is a false belief.

Our pursuit of happiness and contentment does not undermine or belittle the pain and struggles of others. Rather, we can continue to empathize and show compassion towards others while simultaneously cultivating our own happiness. Both our happiness and empathy towards others are meant to coexist harmoniously and be in balance. By finding joy and fulfillment in our lives, we can gain the strength and resilience necessary to tackle challenging situations and even extend help to those around us who may be struggling.

Acknowledging our needs does not entail shutting people out, however, a narcissistic family structure will manipulate the story and blame us for abandoning the family when we are simply setting boundaries on what we can no longer accept. They are, in essence, rejecting our need for equal treatment and using gaslighting to convince us that we are at fault by demanding that we adhere to their regulations without any consideration for how we desire to be treated in return.

We all have tried to communicate our limits and boundaries with our narcissistic family system more times than we can count. Each time that we did this, we offered them the opportunity for a balanced and healthy relationship with us. However, even though we gave them the key, they chose to throw it away and then accused us of locking the door.

It's easy to feel guilty for prioritizing our own happiness and well-being when our blood family has instilled detrimental limiting beliefs within us. We may believe that nurturing our happiness equals ignoring someone else's troubles or that by living their lives for them we will help them fix their problems or alleviate the pain. But this couldn't be further from the truth.

We are all distinct individuals with our own agency over our lives. While we may have the power to offer assistance, comfort, or empathy to others, we cannot live their lives for them.

You can lead a horse to water, but you cannot force it to drink. You can offer the horse a drink and take one for yourself when you're thirsty, but you cannot let the horse's frustrations stop you from quenching your own thirst. If the horse refuses to drink and kicks you every time you get near the water when you get thirsty, that is a dangerous horse.

By accepting that we are not responsible for fixing everything, we can prioritize our own well-being and find joy in our own lives. This doesn't mean ignoring someone else's troubles or refusing to help when we can. Instead, it means taking care of ourselves so that we can better equip ourselves to help others.

Our own happiness is valid and important, and we deserve to find joy and fulfillment in our lives. We should strive to remind ourselves that we can't control the actions or emotions of others and focusing on our own happiness does not mean we are ignoring or neglecting problems. Instead, it means that we are taking care of ourselves, and setting healthy boundaries that allow us to have the extra energy and resources that we may sometimes need to allocate to others as best as we can. Healthy relationships are not built on a foundation of sacrificing needs to please one another, but rather on honoring each others needs and encouraging each person to thrive in their own authenticity.

Journal Prompts

- What do I value most in my life?
- What do I need to feel fulfilled and content?
- What activities bring me the most joy and satisfaction?
- What do I need in order to feel safe and secure?
- What drains my energy and makes me feel unfulfilled?
- What are my core emotional needs?
- What did I always want to do, but never did? What is stopping me from doing it now? How can I fulfill this unmet need?

The Lessons Learned

Explore the various paths that lead to feeling good and choose the one that resonates with you the most. Fulfill your needs by getting to know yourself rather than relying on others. Listen to the voice of your inner child, and as you do, reassure them, saying, "I've got this. I'm in charge now."

Happiness is a fundamental human right, something that everyone deserves to experience. Recognizing our worthiness of happiness and actively working to cultivate it is what living is all about.

You are here, right now, with every breath you take, with every sunrise, a new journey awaits.

Trust that with every small step you take, you are chipping away at the mountain of your struggles. Instead of fixating on the destination, cherish the little moments of joy along the way. Amidst the chaos, you may discover treasures of gratitude waiting to be uncovered.

Chapter 18

Beyond What You Know

Trust The Hero's Journey

The journey of a hero is often depicted as a solitary one, where the hero must stand up against seemingly insurmountable odds to overcome challenges and triumph over evil. This journey is filled with trials and tribulations, and the hero must rely on their inner strength, courage, and determination to push through.

The hero's journey typically begins with a call that only they have the power to answer. This call marks the beginning of the hero's journey, and it sets the stage for facing th unknown where challenges and obstacles will have to be faced.

These obstacles may include battles, solving riddles, and navigating treacherous landscapes. The hero must use their skills and wits to overcome these challenges, and they must also rely on their inner strength and determination to see them through.

As the hero progresses on their journey, they encounter a series of mentors and allies who offer guidance and support. These mentors and allies may be wise old sages, skilled warriors, or powerful magic users, and they provide the hero with the knowledge and skills they need to succeed.

The hero's journey reaches its climax when they reach the final showdown with the primary antagonist, who represents the embodiment of evil. The hero must use everything they have learned on their journey to defeat this enemy and restore balance to the world.

The journey of a hero is not an easy one, but it is one that is filled with purpose and meaning. It is a journey of self-discovery and personal growth, where the hero learns about themselves and their own capabilities, and in the end, they come out wiser, stronger and braver.

The hero's journey is not just a story or a metaphor, it is a reality for those who have been assigned the role of the scapegoat in a narcissistic family system. The challenges and struggles that come with this role can be overwhelming and it can feel like the odds are stacked against us. However, our journey is a story of survival, resilience, self-discovery, and personal growth. This is the stuff that true heroes are made of.

The hero's journey teaches us that we have the inner strength and determination to push through these struggles and overcome the obstacles that stand in our way. It teaches us that we are capable of facing our fears, and that we can find the courage to stand up for ourselves and our needs.

The hero's journey also teaches us that we are not alone in our struggles, and that we can find allies and mentors to support us along the way.

As we continue on our journey, we learn more about ourselves and our own capabilities. We learn to trust ourselves and our instincts, and we learn to find the strength and courage to push through the struggles and obstacles that stand in our way.

We Are All Made of Light and Shadow: Love Yourself As a Whole, Not a Half

Learning to find peace within yourself requires a deep exploration of your authentic self. It involves embracing and integrating both the light and shadow aspects of your being. Recognize your strengths, talents, and positive qualities that deserve acknowledgment and celebration. Simultaneously, acknowledge the shadow elements within you—your vulnerabilities, flaws, and weaknesses—and accept them as part of your journey toward healing and growth.

By accepting and integrating all parts of yourself, you can foster a sense of wholeness and authenticity. Embracing your true self means embracing your complexities, understanding that no one is perfect, and that imperfections are a part of the shared human experience. This journey allows you to transcend the limited narratives that were imposed upon you and discover your own unique identity, free from the confines of external judgments.

Remember, you are more than the role assigned to you by a dysfunctional family system. You are multidimensional with the capacity for growth, self-love, and self-acceptance. By acknowledging your worth and honoring your true essence, you can embark on a path of self-discovery, empowerment, and genuine love for yourself.

Speak Lovingly to Yourself

Learning to speak lovingly to yourself is a vital aspect of cultivating self-love and self-acceptance. The way we talk to ourselves internally has a profound impact on our self-perception, self-esteem, and overall well-being. When you have experienced being scapegoated and unloved within a narcissistic family system, it is even more crucial to counteract the negative narratives that have been imposed upon you.

To foster self love, it is essential to consciously shift your internal dialogue to a more loving and compassionate tone. Instead of engaging in self-criticism or perpetuating the harmful beliefs about yourself, make a deliberate choice to speak to yourself with kindness, understanding, and nurturing words. Treat yourself as you would treat someone you deeply care about.

Practice reframing negative thoughts and replace them with positive ones. When self-judgment arises, consciously challenge those thoughts and replace them with self-compassionate statements. For example, if you catch yourself thinking, "I hate myself" or "I'm so stupid," pause and reframe those thoughts into more supportive and loving messages such as, "Other people's reactions to my boundaries are not in my control", or "I'm allowed to make mistakes" and " I'm allowed to change my mind."

With Every Decision You Make, Always Choose Self-Love

Choosing self-love does not mean that you are selfish. In fact, when you genuinely practice self-love, the positive energy and light you cultivate within yourself naturally extends to those around you. Loving yourself authentically empowers you to support and uplift others on their own journeys of self-growth and self-discovery.

Self-love is not synonymous with being self-centered. In truth, being self-centered often stems from a lack of self-love. When someone is deeply insecure and lacks self-esteem, they may feel the need to elevate themselves by bringing others down. This behavior is rooted in a scarcity mindset, believing that there is not enough success or happiness to go around. However, true self-love is based on the understanding that there is an abundance of love, joy, and success available to everyone. Love is limitless. When you understand this, you begin to understand that you do not have to choose between loving yourself, or loving someone else, and if someone is expecting you to do that, than you are not in a healthy relationship.

When you find yourself at a crossroads, grappling with feelings of guilt, shame, doubt, and confusion, it's important to remember that choosing self-love doesn't have to be complicated. There's one fundamental question you can ask yourself to guide your decisions: "What is the move I can make that reflects my own self-love and self-respect?"

Making a conscious choice to love yourself is a profound affirmation of your inherent worth. Despite the mistreatment and neglect you may have endured, acknowledging your value and deservingness of love is a transformative act. It signifies a commitment to prioritize your well-being and embrace self-love as a guiding principle in your life.

I Love Myself, I Trust Myself

Affirmations of self-love are powerful tools for nurturing a positive self-image and promoting self-acceptance. By regularly repeating affirmations such as "I love myself unconditionally," "I am worthy of love and respect," or "I embrace all parts of myself with love," you reinforce positive beliefs about yourself and challenge negative self-perceptions.

Affirmations serve as reminders of your inherent worthiness of love and act as a counterbalance to the negative messages ingrained in your subconscious from past experiences. Through consistent repetition, these affirmations help rewire your thought patterns, replacing self-doubt and self-criticism with self-love and self-compassion.

When faced with challenges or setbacks, affirmations can be especially helpful in reminding yourself that you did what was necessary to protect and respect yourself, rather than engaging in endless rumination. They reinforce the understanding that you made choices aligned with your well-being and that you can trust yourself to make sound decisions.

My personal favorite has always been "I love myself, I trust myself." In moments of self-doubt, loneliness, guilt, shame, or fear, this mantra has kept me going and continues to do so today.

Taking Back What Is Rightfully Ours

For too long, I searched outside of myself for a sense of belonging and validation, only to realize that the home I yearned for was already within me. I am my own sanctuary, capable of cultivating a life filled with joy, purpose, and love independently. By setting healthy boundaries and honoring my needs, I've created a safe and nurturing environment where I can thrive and grow.

Although some may try to invalidate my experiences and rewrite history to suit their own narrative, I know my truth, and that's sufficient. I am no longer bound by other people's denial and gaslighting of my reality. I do not look for their validation to heal anymore. Instead, I choose to craft a future aligned with my highest good.

While people are free to believe in anything they wish, we also have the freedom to choose who becomes part of our world based on whether their values and beliefs enrich and empower us or diminish and weaken us.

I am at peace with this, recognizing that other people's choices and beliefs are not my burden to carry anymore.

What matters now is finding our place of belonging within ourselves and our environment. This journey takes time and patience, but each small step brings us closer to our goal. It's a beautiful feeling to have the agency to choose the direction of our future and the people we allow into our lives.

The journey of the scapegoat is brutally difficult, yet through it, we discover our deep well of strength, resilience, and power. Our past does not determine our future; we hold the power to choose our next direction. Letting go of what we cannot control and focusing on creating the life we desire leads us toward peace and justice.

Embarking on this journey requires courage. You have already shown bravery by stepping onto this path, and you must continue to believe in yourself as you move forward. Make yourself the central figure of your story. You decide. You set the rules.

The next chapter is yours to write.

www.ingramcontent.com/pod-product-compliance
Lightning Source LLC
Chambersburg PA
CBHW031424150426
43191CB00006B/386